Elvis Presley

with profiles of
Muddy Waters
and Mick Jagger

World Book, Inc.
a Scott Fetzer company
Chicago

BIOGRAPHICAL ⊕ CONNECTIONS

Writer: Susan M. Doll.

World Book, Inc.
233 N. Michigan Ave.
Chicago, IL 60601

For information about other World Book publications, visit our Web site at **www.worldbook.com** or call **1-800-WORLDBK (967-5325)**.
For information about sales to schools and libraries, call **1-800-975-3250 (United States)**, or **1-800-837-5365 (Canada)**.

Library of Congress Cataloging-in-Publication Data

Doll, Susan, 1954-
  Elvis Presley: with profiles of Muddy Waters and Mick Jagger.
    p. cm. -- (Biographical connections)
  Summary: "A biography of Elvis Presley, with profiles of two prominent individuals, who are associated through the influences they had on one another, the successes they achieved, or the goals they worked toward. Includes recommended readings and web sites"--Provided by publisher.
  Includes bibliographical references (p.   ) and index.
  ISBN-13: 978-0-7166-1823-2
  ISBN-10: 0-7166-1823-0
  1. Presley, Elvis, 1935-1977--Juvenile literature. 2. Rock musicians--United States--Biography--Juvenile literature. 3. Muddy Waters, 1915-1983--Juvenile literature. 4. Jagger, Mick--Juvenile literature. I. World Book, Inc. II. Title. III. Series.
  ML3929.D65 2007
  782.42166092--dc22
  [B]
                                    2006015007

Printed in the United States of America
1 2 3 4 5 10 09 08 07 06

Contents

Acknowledgments

The publisher gratefully acknowledges the following sources for the photographs in this volume. All maps are the exclusive property of World Book, Inc.

Cover	© Binder, Howe Productions/The Kobal Collection
	© Terry Cryer, Corbis
	© Richard Upper, Redferns
7	© Terry Cryer, Corbis
8	WORLD BOOK map
10	© Karl R. Josker
12	© GAB Archives/Redferns
14	© Michael Ochs Archives
19	© BMI/Michael Ochs Archives
21	© Agence France-Presse
25	© Michael Ochs Archives
26	© GEMS/Redferns
28	© Elvis Presley Enterprises, Inc. Used with permission.
33	© GAB Archives/Redferns
37	© Michael Ochs Archives
38	© GAB Archives/Redferns
42	© Elvis Presley Enterprises, Inc. Used with Permission.
47	© Photos 12
50	© Michael Ochs Archives
55	© Elvis Presley Enterprises, Inc. Used with permission.
62	© Michael Ochs Archives
68	© GAB Archives/Redferns
71-80	© Michael Ochs Archives
85	AP/Wide World

Preface

Biographical Connections takes a contextual approach in presenting the lives of important people. In each volume, there is a biography of a central figure. This biography is preceded and followed by pro-files of other individuals whose lifework connects in some way to that of the central figure. The three subjects are associated through the influences they had on one another, the successes they achieved, or the goals they worked toward. The series includes men and women from around the world and throughout history in a variety of fields.

The three performers spotlighted in this book were all innovators of rock 'n' roll music. They either integrated diverse types of music into an exciting new sound or synthesized their musical influences into a distinctive style. Their music shows a progression in which the Southern-based blues of Muddy Waters (the volume's first profile) became an element of Elvis Presley's rockabilly and then provided a solid basis to the rock 'n' roll of Mick Jagger, the lead singer of the Rolling Stones. Also, the controversial performing style of Elvis Presley (the central biography in this volume) opened the door for the stage antics of Jagger (the last profile in this volume), while the sense of rebellion attributed to Presley was fully embraced by those who followed in his path, including the Rolling Stones.

Rock 'n' roll music is a raucous cultural melting pot. It integrates a variety of musical styles from different cultural sources into a sound that is unique yet retains the echoes of its influences. It is a music that characterized the second half of the 1900's—fast-paced, loud, intense, and driven by technology.

Though it would be impossible to trace the origins of rock 'n' roll to one source, the three musicians in this book all contributed to the development of this exciting form of music. Blues singer Muddy Waters came up from the Mississippi Delta to Chicago, where he added an electric guitar to his sexually charged blues music. This instrument would become an essential ingredient of rock 'n' roll. Like Waters, Presley was born in Mississippi, where he absorbed the sounds of the South, including the blues, rhythm and blues, and country-western. During the 1950's, when rock 'n' roll exploded into America's consciousness, Presley's fast-paced rockabilly developed into the standard rock style. Not only was Presley's music electric but so was his performing style. He was constantly in motion on the stage, expressing himself through movement as well as song. Across the Atlantic, the hard-driving rock 'n' roll of Britain's Rolling Stones was heavily influenced by the electric blues of such American musicians as Muddy Waters. And like Presley, Mick Jagger, the lead singer of the Rolling Stones, became an expressive on-stage performer known for his charismatic presence and his sensual, expressive moves. Outspoken and outrageous, Jagger and the Rolling Stones embodied the rebellious spirit of rock 'n' roll that was once attributed to Elvis Presley.

A hint of the importance of these three figures is revealed through their nicknames, or titles. Muddy Waters is sometimes called "The King of the Electric Blues," Elvis Presley has been "The King of Rock 'n' Roll" for five decades, and the Rolling Stones are frequently labeled "The Greatest Rock 'n' Roll Band in the World." A look at the lives and careers of these musicians shows how they earned their titles. ■

Muddy Waters (1915–1983)

"The Blues had a baby and they named the baby Rock And Roll."

Muddy Waters, lyric from the song, "The Blues Had a Baby and They Named It Rock And Roll"

Muddy Waters is the most important originator of urban blues, which has also been called the Chicago blues. This type of blues music was created when an electrically amplified guitar was added to traditional Southern blues. Blues music had already elevated the guitar to a position of prominence, but the electric guitar added volume. It also modernized the blues. The urban blues of Muddy Waters and others indirectly influenced the rock 'n' roll sound that emerged during the 1950's, including the music of American singer Elvis Presley. But it was Muddy Waters himself who *directly* influenced the English rock groups and singers of the classic rock era, including Mick Jagger and the Rolling Stones, Eric Clapton, and Eric Burdon and the Animals, as well as American guitar legend Jimi Hendrix.

EARLY LIFE

Muddy Waters was born McKinley Morganfield near Rolling Fork, Mississippi, on April 4, 1915. The son of Ollie Morganfield and Berta Jones, the little boy had a hard life by today's standards. When he was about 3 years old, his mother died, and he was given to his grandmother to raise. This was his mother's mother, Della Jones, who lived in a sharecropper's cabin on the Stovall plantation in Clarksdale, Mississippi.

Both Rolling Fork and Clarksdale are in the Mississippi Delta, a bowl-shaped stretch of land that reaches from Memphis in the north

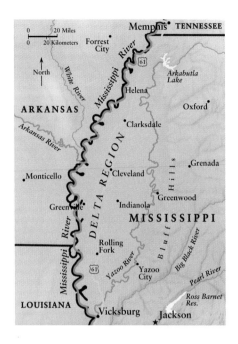

to Vicksburg, Mississippi, in the south. From east to west, it lies between the Yazoo and Mississippi rivers. The mighty Mississippi River dumps soil, ground rock, animal remains, and tree trunks along the Delta. These deposits form new land that is rich and fertile.

The Delta is a region defined not only by its geography but also by its cultural characteristics. The region gave birth to a distinct form of blues music called the Delta blues. Because of its rich culture, the Delta is steeped in legend and folklore, and much of it swirls around the blues.

Clarksdale is about 100 miles (160 kilometers) north of Rolling Fork on Highway 61, one of the most famous routes in America's popular culture history. U.S. Highway 61 once ran from New Orleans all the way to the United States/Canada border. It was an important north-south connection in the days before the interstate highway system. Many African Americans seeking a better life traveled from the South along Highway 61 to go north to Chicago. The road is also known to blues fans as the "Blues Highway" because several blues artists wrote songs about Highway 61, and many who found fame outside of the Delta followed the legendary route out of the South. That Muddy Waters was born and grew up near Highway 61 is as much fate as fact.

The boy's grandmother gave little McKinley the nickname that overshadowed his given name. As a small child, he liked to play along the creek bank, where he frequently could be found caked in mud. The creek was not far from the cabin where he lived with his grandmother and his uncle. Originally built as a hunter's cabin some time before the American Civil War (1861–1865), the house had a kitchen and three tiny rooms. There was no electrical power or running water. It was a typical sharecropper's or tenant-farmer's home of the period.

When Waters was in the third grade, he had to quit school to go to work in the cotton fields. Cotton and corn had been the major crops in the Delta since before the Civil War, and most of the region's

Muddy Waters was born in the Mississippi Delta, a bowl-shaped stretch of land that reaches from Memphis in the north to Vicksburg, Mississippi, in the south. From east to west, it lies between the Yazoo and Mississippi rivers.

poor—whether white or black—had been working the fields to feed their families for decades. For about 50 cents to 75 cents per day, Waters plowed the fields at the beginning of the season and then picked either cotton or corn when the crop was ready. It was back-breaking work, but for many poor blacks living in America's rural South at the time, there were few alternatives. As Muddy Waters said years later in an interview, "I paid my dues, I'll tell you that."[1]

THE AFRICAN HERITAGE OF THE BLUES

The blues can be traced to the African people who were taken from their land to work as slaves beginning in colonial times. Separated from the musical and oral traditions of their native regions, African slaves in America found they had two places where they could express these traditions freely: in the fields where they worked and in the churches where they worshiped.

Spirituals, work songs, and field hollers (short, improvised solo calls and wails) were a way for African slaves to lighten the load of their task during long work hours. They were also a means of communication: of telling stories, passing along news, and releasing frustrations.

After the Civil War, early blues carried on the tradition of voicing African American aspirations and experiences. Many blues lyrics reflect loneliness or sorrow, but others declare a humorous or defiant reaction to life's troubles.

While working in the fields, Muddy Waters listened to the other field hands as they sang traditional work songs or shouted out field hollers. He also heard spirituals and gospel music in the local Baptist church, which he and his grandmother attended regularly. Sometimes a neighbor let him listen to recordings by Southern blues artists such as Blind Lemon Jefferson, Texas Alexander, Barbecue Bob, and Blind Blake. Sometimes Waters was able to buy records, and sometimes he listened to recordings on the jukebox. Throughout his childhood, Waters was surrounded by the music of the South.

Around the age of 7, Muddy Waters received a harmonica for Christmas. Though he practiced often, he did not master the instrument until he was about 13. Along the way, he beat on cans, fooled around with an old accordion, and played a Jew's harp, before he and a friend began to make music together. Waters played the harmonica while his friend picked out the blues on the guitar. His friend Scott Bohanner, whom Waters would later call Scott Brown or Scott Bowhandle in interviews, began to teach Waters the guitar. By the time he was 17, Waters was the better guitar player. The pair played at local parties, fish fries, and juke joints. (A *juke joint*, or *juke house*, is a makeshift bar where locals gather on weekends.) When his grandmother heard him play the blues on the harmonica and guitar, she warned him that he was playing the Devil's music, because the lifestyle of the juke joints was rough. People drank, gambled, and partied into the wee hours.

Waters began to shape his personal style of blues by listening to Eddie James, Jr. (better known as Son House), and the legendary Robert Johnson. Son House was an especially big influence. House lived and worked on a plantation that was some distance from Stovall, but he traveled a lot, working the juke joints and fish fries. Waters went to hear House play as often as he could. He studied the master bluesman's style by watching his hands and fingers closely. He also listened to House's recordings.

Waters saw Robert Johnson perform only once or twice, but he learned some of his songs from recordings. Johnson had played traditional blues around the Delta in the late 1920's and early 1930's. Johnson left the area for awhile and when he returned, his guitar playing had improved dramatically. His music had evolved into a new kind of sound. Johnson was now leading the blues in a new direction, instead of following the traditional style. In 1938, Johnson died while still in his 20's. Witnesses claimed he had been murdered. Because he died so young, a legend was spun around his short life and

Muddy Waters lived in this sharecropper's cabin on the Stovall Plantation in Clarksdale, Mississippi, from the time he was a small boy until he set out at age 28 to seek his fortune as a blues musician in Chicago. This photo shows what remained of the cabin in 1995.

tragic death. According to folklore, Johnson sold his soul to the Devil in exchange for a mastery of the blues. The bargain supposedly took place at the junction of Highway 61 and Highway 49. The legend undoubtedly sprang in part from Johnson's song "Crossroad Blues," in which the singer goes "to the crossroad" and begs the Lord to "have mercy [and] save poor Bob."

Both House and Johnson played the guitar using the *bottleneck*, or slide, technique. This was the technique that Waters learned and then mastered. In this style of playing, the musician uses the neck from a broken bottle to slide down the strings on the guitar neck as he plays. He might substitute a pocket knife or a butter knife for the bottleneck, but the effect is the same. It produces a metallic, wailing sound that is more expressive than standard guitar-picking. The style could be as expressive as vocals, and it was often used to complement, or "answer," the singer as he or she belted out the lyrics. The style was responsible for elevating the guitar from a backup instrument that provided rhythm to a lead instrument.

A DRIVE "TO BE KNOWN"

As Waters grew into adulthood, his life was defined by work in the fields during the weekdays and playing music on the weekends. He continued to live with his grandmother, and sometimes supplemented their income by trapping animals and selling the pelts, or by making and selling moonshine (home-made alcohol). For two or three years, he ran his own juke joint, which offered moonshine, music, and mayhem. By the late 1930's, he had become a well-known blues musician around the Delta, and he began to play for white audiences at events and parties.

Waters liked the recognition that being a bluesman brought to him, and he wanted to make something of his life. He worked hard at mastering the blues, especially the slide technique. Years later, he told an interviewer, ". . . to master [the slide technique] you've got to know what you're doing there. You've got to know blues to go down in and get some of it and get out of it, you know. I had it in my mind even then to either play music or preach or do something that I would be known, that people would know me. I kept that on my mind. I wanted

Muddy Waters began recording with Chess Records in 1947. Waters is shown here in an early Chess publicity photo.

to be a known person. All my life. That's what I worked for. I wanted to be internationally known. And I worked on it, from when I was a kid up."[2]

In 1940, Waters took a major step in that direction when he moved to St. Louis, Missouri, for a few months. He hoped to start a more professional musical career there, but he had only limited success. Unable to make enough money to support himself, he returned to the Delta.

The following year, he began playing for broadcasts on radio station KFFA from Helena, Arkansas. Two blues artists who had played at Waters's juke joint, Sonny Boy Williamson II (Aleck "Rice" Miller) and Robert Lockwood, Jr., organized a live blues program that aired from noon till 12:15 p.m. on workdays. Called "King Biscuit Time," the show coincided with the lunch breaks of the field hands. Williamson and Lockwood invited Waters to perform on their program one Saturday afternoon. The exposure increased his regional recognition and gave him a taste of the musician's life.

Also in 1941, two folk-music historians, Alan Lomax, who was white, and John Work III, who was African American, traveled to the Delta looking for Robert Johnson in order to record him. They were also interested in recording regional music from different parts of the South for the Library of Congress. Lomax and Work were informed that Johnson had died a few years earlier. Several locals told them to look up Muddy Waters, who was playing regularly with a group of older bluesmen at the time. Lomax and Work found him on the Stovall plantation and recorded him while he played a steel-bodied acoustic guitar and sang "I Be's Troubled" and "Country Blues." The former was a song Waters had written after hearing a gospel song, and the latter was a tune based on Johnson's "Walkin' Blues," which Waters told Lomax he wrote while changing a flat tire. Lomax played the recordings back to Waters, making it the first time the musician had ever heard his recorded voice. Waters was paid $20 (about $265 today) for the recordings, and later he received two copies of the discs. The next year, Lomax returned and made two more recordings. Though not commercial releases, the 1941 recordings marked the first recording of Muddy Waters, now a professional musician.

GOIN' TO CHICAGO

Many rural Southerners migrated north during and after World War II (1939–1945), using the prosperity of the time to seek better employment opportunities. In May 1943, Waters moved to Chicago, intending to find a day job so that he could pursue a musical career in the clubs in the evenings. Upon arrival, Waters stayed first with friends and then with relatives on the South Side of the city while looking for a job and learning his way around. He quickly found work at the Joanna Western Mills paper mill. Six months later, he was able to rent his own apartment.

Waters selected Chicago as a destination because the city had been a major recording center for blues music since the 1920's, when the first wave of black blues musicians arrived. However, by the 1940's, commercial blues music in Chicago had become smoother and glossier to appeal to an urban, Northern audience. The raw country or Delta influence had been eliminated in favor of a more sophisticated style. At the time, music in Chicago was dominated by jazz artists, such as Nat "King" Cole and Billy Eckstine. The big swing bands, such as those of Count Basie, Tommy Dorsey, and Duke Ellington, were all the rage on the radio stations. Big-band swing music combines a fast, sophisticated dance tempo with elaborate instrumental arrangements. The smoother blues found in Chicago probably resulted from the influence of these other styles of music.

Waters's start in the Chicago music scene was modest. He began playing house parties on weekends. The premiere blues musicians in Chicago during the 1940's were guitarists Big Bill Broonzy, Lonnie Johnson, and Tampa Red, and pianists Big Maceo and Memphis Slim. Broonzy became a major booster of Waters's. He encouraged him to pursue a blues career but, most importantly, he introduced the recent arrival to club owners and other people in the music scene.

Waters found work playing with Sonny Boy Williamson I (John

Lee Williamson) at the Plantation, a South Side tavern. He soon realized he needed amplification to be heard over the noisy crowds that patronized the bars in Chicago. Many other blues artists, including Jimmy Rogers, had already added amplifiers to their guitars. In 1944, he got an inexpensive electric guitar from his uncle. The new instrument expanded his sound but did not change his basic style. He continued to use a sawed-off neck from a bottle as a slide along the guitar frets, just as he and his mentors had done in the Delta. Waters brought a taste of the Delta to the big-city blues by adding a hard *backbeat*. (Backbeat, one of the defining characteristics of rock 'n' roll, is a percussion style where a strong rhythmic accent is sounded on the second and fourth beats of the bar.) With a voice that could stretch from a guttural baritone to a pure falsetto, Waters sang with a raw, rough edge, shouting, howling, or running the lyrics together to create the fast-phrased vocal style that became one of his trademarks. He formed a trio with Jimmy Rogers (on harmonica, later switching to guitar) and guitarist Claude "Blue Smitty" Smith. Smith taught Waters additional techniques on the guitar, such as finger-fretting, or playing without the slide, on his solos. Their sound evolved into the style later known as the Chicago blues.

During the 1950's, Waters played regularly at the best blues clubs in Chicago. The Muddy Waters Band is shown at the Zanzibar Club in Chicago in 1954. Waters, left, *is on guitar, Otis Spann is on piano, and Jimmy Rogers,* right, *is on guitar.*

CHESS RECORDS

In 1947, Waters got an opportunity to record that helped him to establish his name and reputation, though it was not his first experience with making records in Chicago. Leonard and Phil Chess, who owned a club on the South Side, bought an interest in Aristocrat Records in Chicago, to record acts that proved popular in their club. In 1950, the brothers would change the name of their company to Chess.

Waters recorded several songs for the Chess brothers before they released Waters's first important disc, "I Can't Be Satisfied" backed by "I Feel Like Going Home," in April 1948. The record sold well in Chicago and gave him and his band the opportunity to play better clubs in the city, such as the Du Drop Lounge and the Boogie Woogie Inn. A short time later, he recorded "Rollin' Stone" with "Walkin' Blues" on the flip side. The record was Chess's first bona fide hit. Later, it would inspire the title of Bob Dylan's song "Like a Rolling Stone," as well as the name of the world's most enduring rock 'n' roll band, the Rolling Stones, and America's premiere popular music magazine, *Rolling Stone*.

By the 1950's, Waters was recording regularly at Chess Records, getting his music played on black radio stations, playing regularly at the best Chicago blues clubs, and touring occasionally across the South and in the East. The work at Chess helped Waters secure the band that firmly established the Chicago blues sound between 1948 and 1952. Little Walter Jacobs became his harmonica player. Jacobs amplified the harmonica, turning it into a serious blues instrument. Jimmy Rogers backed him on guitar. Rogers and Jacobs were also from the Delta and instinctively knew what Waters wanted with his music. Rogers, Jacobs, and Waters made up the core band, especially on the road. Willie Dixon, who played bass and wrote many of the band's songs, joined them in the Chess studio. Years later, Waters described his Chicago blues to interviewer James Rooney. "I had it in my mind I wanted to do this particular thing. I wanted to play close 'round Son House, between Son and Robert [Johnson], and I got in there with it. My particular style is based on their style, but is not exactly like them.

I wanted to play between those two."[3] The Chicago blues style innovated by Waters and the band spread to Memphis, Detroit, and even back to the Mississippi Delta.

As the 1950's progressed, band members came and went. Other musicians that played with Waters in the 1950's included Elgin Evans on drums; Junior Wells, Big Walter Horton, and James Cotton on harmonica; Buddy Guy on guitar; and Otis Spann on piano. Spann grew very close to Waters, who affectionately referred to him as his brother or half-brother, though the two were not related. Important recordings from the period include "Hoochie Coochie Man" and "I Just Want to Make Love to You." Both songs made the list of Top-Ten best-selling records on the rhythm and blues (r & b) charts. These charts were listed in such music-industry trade magazines as *Billboard* and *Cashbox* and were an important way for record companies and performers to monitor the popularity of their records. Each style of music had its own chart, and the 10 best-selling records on each chart were called the *Top Ten*. To have a Top-Ten hit opened other doors for musicians and singers that helped to advance their careers.

Waters heightened the electrically charged energy of these songs with a sexual intensity when he performed them before an audience. On such songs as "Got My Mojo Working" and "Mannish Boy," Waters would thrust his hips and quiver his body in the "hootchy-kootchy" way that Elvis Presley and Mick Jagger would adopt years later. Presley even went on to perform "Got My Mojo Working" in concert; the Rolling Stones would record and perform "I Just Want to Make Love to You," "Mannish Boy," and other Muddy Waters songs.

In addition to the sexual bravado Waters exhibited in these and many other songs, he often made colorful references to voodoo in his lyrics: "mojo," "black cat bone," and "John the Conqueror Root" are allusions to voodoo spells, charms, and superstitions that can be traced to the blues' African roots. These themes, as well as the more traditional blues themes of heartbreak, frustration, weariness, and loneliness, formed the foundation of a sound that Muddy Waters made uniquely his own.

CHANGING TIMES, CHANGING TASTES

As Waters was recording and touring in the early- to mid-1950's, Elvis Presley combined blues and *rhythm and blues* (blues-based rock 'n' roll) with country-western and pop music to create a new sound. Rock 'n' roll became the sensation of the nation. It shone a spotlight on the music of black musicians, and white radio stations began to play blues and rhythm and blues. During this time, some of Waters's records were played on white radio stations. However, his raw blues sound appealed to few rock 'n' roll fans, and his record sales never reached the numbers of the new rockabilly, r & b, and rock 'n' roll artists. Even young African American music fans seemed to prefer the r & b and *doo-wop* (catchy tunes with simple rhythms and vocal harmonies) that began to dominate the radio airwaves. Just as Chess Records released his first album, *The Best of Muddy Waters*, his performance engagements began to dwindle.

However, Muddy Waters was becoming extremely popular in England. American blues records had begun appearing in that country after World War II (1939–1945), and teen-agers grew increasingly fascinated by this completely American form of music. By the mid-1950's, English singers and bands were incorporating blues influences into their own music. They were also interested in American folk music and Dixieland jazz. Promoters wanted to book the traditional American music acts into the clubs and touring circuits of England. Big Bill Broonzy was asked to go to England by one promoter. Broonzy recommended that Muddy Waters go. In 1958, Waters and Otis Spann traveled to England, bringing the Chicago blues to another country. It was the last kindness Broonzy did for Waters; Broonzy died in August of that year.

Waters and Spann opened in Leeds, England, but the engagement did not go as planned. The other act they were performing with was a Dixieland jazz band, and the audience was not expecting Waters's loud, hard-driving Chicago blues. They were expecting music like Big Bill Broonzy's. The next day, the newspapers reported on the pair's "screaming guitar" and "howling piano," though witnesses who were there claimed these reports were exaggerations. However, as the pair continued to play across England, and Waters adjusted his sound

Leonard Chess, far left, one of the founders of Chess Records, recorded some of the best blues and r & b artists in Chicago. Muddy Waters (in white shirt) is on guitar, Little Walter is on harmonica, and Bo Diddley, right, is on guitar.

to the smaller, less noisy clubs and venues, the tour became a success.

With the 1958 tour of England, Muddy Waters began to develop a white audience. British musicians, promoters, and music club owners grew more interested in the music. Guitarist Alexis Korner and Cyril Davies, who owned a club, were among those inspired by Muddy Waters. Considered critical in the development of blues in England, the pair fostered the careers of British rockers Mick Jagger, Keith Richards, Brian Jones, Eric Burdon, and Jimmy Page. Through them, the Chicago blues became a major influence on the blues-tinged English rock bands, such as the Rolling Stones, the Yardbirds, and the Animals.

When Waters and Spann returned from England, the bluesmen discovered that the European engagement had attracted the attention of American promoters and enthusiasts interested in folk and jazz. The 1960 Newport Jazz Festival booked Waters and his full band to perform at the fest in early July. They were a major sensation. Not only did Chess Records issue an album of the live performance, but the U.S. Information Service shot film footage of the band for a documentary. Riding the largest wave of success since his career began, Waters returned to England in 1962 and 1963. By this time, the young British rock bands were not just influenced by Muddy Waters, they were completely in awe of him.

When the British bands began making their first tours of America, many of them eagerly told the press about the influence of bluesmen like Waters on their music. Despite his appearance at Newport, and the growing interest of young white audiences, the mainstream American public and newspapers were largely uninformed about this style of music. When the Beatles arrived in America, they revealed that they were going to look up Muddy Waters and Bo Diddley. An ignorant reporter asked, "Muddy Waters. Where's that?" A stunned Paul McCartney responded, "Don't you know who your own famous people are here?"[4]

In 1964, the Rolling Stones, when they first came to Chicago, went directly to Chess Records to record where their idol Muddy Waters—the man to whom they owed their band's name—had recorded. The Stones even paid homage to this temple of sound with their song, "2120 South Michigan Avenue" (the address of Chess Records).

The respect of the British bands for American blues generated more interest in Muddy Waters among young white audiences. In Chicago, students from the University of Chicago came to the clubs to hear the bluesmen play. Also venturing to the South Side to hear Waters and his peers were young white musicians Mike Bloomfield and Paul Butterfield. Later, they would form an important rock-blues group called the Paul Butterfield Blues Band. Muddy Waters often credited the Rolling Stones, and even the Beatles, with exposing his music to white audiences. With white audiences buying his records, white venues and touring circuits opened for him and other bluesmen. Waters and his band toured colleges and festivals. As rock 'n' roll and blues music grew closer together, the blues performers were booked as opening acts for rock groups in clubs and coffee houses. Later, Waters reasoned that "my kind of music had to be exposed to 'em [white audiences in America]. And, it wasn't exposed to 'em until after the Rolling Stones and the Beatles. That's a funny damn thing. Had to get somebody from out of another country to let my white kids over here know where we stand."[5] In analyzing his statement, it is clear that he is not blaming audiences for not knowing about him, or the blues. Instead, it was the music industry—the radio stations, the touring circuits, the recording companies, the record stores—

who kept musicians like him in the background because of racism and their own ignorance of his music.

During the late 1960's, Chess Records suggested that Waters venture into a more modern sound. For an album called *Muddy, Brass and the Blues*, they added brass horns and an organ to his music, which were not instruments in sync with the Muddy Waters sound. Next, Chess wanted Waters to adapt his blues to psychedelic rock using technology that created music that could not be re-created in live performances. The resulting album, *Electric Mud*, had a memorable title and back cover photo (in which Waters is depicted wearing a white toga, with his hair styled in an elaborate pompadour), but the music was forgettable. These attempts to force Waters into a modern, rock-influenced sound were unsuccessful musically. Waters resented these efforts to change the blues in general and his sound in particular. Also, he could not see the sense in making music that could not be produced on stage in front of audiences. This contradicted the soul of the blues, which is to relate directly to the problems, heartaches, and troubles of people. That connection is best made when the blues are performed live.

BLUES FATHER

A much better pairing of rock and the blues occurred when several white rock musicians joined Waters and Otis Spann for the double album *Fathers and Sons*, released in 1969. Paul Butterfield, Mike Bloomfield, and Donald "Duck" Dunn (of Memphis r & b group Booker T. & the MGs and later the Blues Brothers) gladly gathered at the Chess studios to play for Waters. The title of the album symbolized the relationship between the white musicians and the "elders"—Muddy Waters and Otis Spann. He was indeed their musical father. The most powerful tunes featured on this album included "Walkin' Thru the Park," "Can't Lose What You Ain't Never Had," "Standin' Round Cryin'," and "Forty Days and Forty Nights."

Fathers and Sons may have been a career highlight for Waters in 1969, but the year also witnessed a low point for the bluesman. On the way home from a concert in October, he was involved in a serious car accident in which the drivers of both the vehicles and a passenger were killed. Waters suffered a broken leg, a sprained back, some broken ribs, and a paralyzed right hand. He was in the hospital for almost three months. Afterward, he remained at home for several more months trying to recuperate. Part of the time he was in bed; part of the time he was on crutches. With the help of physical therapy, he was able to walk and use his right hand again. But he never played the guitar with the same skill he had before. The death of Otis Spann—his close friend and collaborator—in 1970 deepened Waters's distress.

By late 1970, Waters had recuperated and returned to the road. Although he played the guitar less, he sang the blues harder. The following year, Chess records sent Waters to London to record with young British artists who had been influenced by him. The record was called *The London Muddy Waters Sessions* and featured Steve Winwood, Mitch Mitchell, Georgie Fame, and Irish blues-rock guitarist Rory Gallagher.

Mick Jagger, lead singer of the Rolling Stones, performs with his idol at the Quiet Knight in Chicago in 1978. The Rolling Stones were named after the Muddy Waters song "Rollin' Stone."

HARD AGAIN

In the 1970's, Waters again found the music scene moving away from the raw, hard Delta blues that he had played and perfected. The style of blues most popular during this time was the type played by B.B. King, whose blues music was not as raw and intense as Waters's. According to Waters, King could sing in "a higher class place" with his style, which Waters thought was more attractive to urban audiences. Waters appeared with his fellow blues artists less and less frequently on the road, but he did play some engagements that were prestigious. For example, he performed at Radio City Music Hall in New York City and music festivals around the world.

The road may have been less inviting to Waters in the 1970's, but the recording studio lured him back. He cut some of his most interesting albums during this period. However, he broke away from Chess Records. The studio had been sold and resold over the years to larger and larger companies. The small, personal approach to running the studio had long since disappeared. He sued Arc Music, which was the part of Chess that published music, because he did not receive the royalty payments that he was owed on his songs. Waters and the company settled out of court. Waters's problems with royalties and receiving proper compensation were not unlike the unfair practices that other African American artists had experienced in the music business. In 1976, he signed a recording contract with Blue Sky Records, which was a division of Columbia.

His contract involved a series of albums to be produced by Johnny Winter, a celebrated white performer from Texas whose sound integrated blues and rock 'n' roll. Winter had met Waters in Austin when Winter was a preteen guitar prodigy. They had worked together in 1974, when they appeared together on the Public Broadcasting System (PBS) music series *Soundstage*. Winter wanted Waters to sing the blues in his old style, but the Texan wanted to use modern recording techniques to cut the albums. He hired back-up musicians whom Waters knew and was comfortable with, such as former band member James Cotton on harmonica and Pinetop Perkins, who had replaced Otis Spann on piano in the early 1970's. Their first album was recorded live in the studio and released in 1977. Titled *Hard Again*, it captured the power of the blues performed live and the authority of an artist who is a master in his field. Waters recorded new material, reworked old standards, and even recut one of the songs he had recorded for Alan Lomax back in 1941. Winter did most of the slide guitar work on the album, because age and the car accident had made it difficult for Waters to play. The album became one of Waters's personal favorites, and it was essential in securing good bookings in America and Europe for his new band.

Other albums produced by Winter followed, including *I'm Ready*, the following year, and *Muddy "Mississippi" Waters Live*, released in 1979, a collection of songs performed at live venues. Winter also produced the last album cut by Waters, titled *King Bee*, in 1980 and released in 1981. Waters won a half dozen Grammy Awards for his music during his career, with three of them awarded for the albums he made with Winter. At the end of the 1970's, Muddy Waters enjoyed the kind of recognition he deserved as the elder statesman of blues. Rock musicians jumped over each other for an opportunity to record with him. In 1976, he was part of the last concert on the "farewell tour" of The Band, an influential American/Canadian folk-rock group of the 1960's and 1970's. This concert was turned into a documentary called *The Last Waltz* (1978). (The Band would reunite several times beginning in the 1980's.) Directed by award-winning American filmmaker Martin Scorsese, the film captures Muddy Waters singing and playing from his soul in one of his later performances.

At the end of his life, Waters became ill with lung cancer. He was preparing to cut another album when he suffered a heart attack at his home in suburban Westmont, Illinois, and died on April 30, 1983. Waters had been married more than once and had several children and grandchildren. At least one of his sons, Big Bill Morganfield, followed in his father's footsteps by playing blues. After his death, Muddy Waters was inducted into the Rock and Roll Hall of Fame (before it opened in Cleveland, Ohio, in 1995) in 1987, and he received a posthumous Grammy Award for Lifetime Achievement in 1992.

Muddy Waters lives on through his music. His creativity and rough, expressive style continue to inspire later generations who carry on the traditions and sounds of the blues that originated in the Mississippi Delta and were fine-tuned in Chicago. As Buddy Guy, currently the elder statesman of the Chicago blues, stated, "Whenever you hear me play, man, there's a part of Muddy Waters, Howlin' Wolf, Little Walter—all those great musicians."[6] ■

Chronology of Presley's life

1935   born on January 8 in Tupelo, Mississippi

1953   makes first record by paying the Memphis Recording Service to record two songs

1954   Memphis Recording Service and Sun Records owner Sam Phillips calls Presley to record; Memphis DJ Dewey Phillips plays Presley's "That's All Right," and the record becomes a local hit; Presley and the Blue Moon Boys perform on the "Grand Ole Opry" radio show in Nashville, Tennessee; the group performs for the first time on the "Louisiana Hayride" radio show in Shreveport

1955   Colonel Tom Parker becomes Presley's manager; RCA buys Presley's contract from Sun Records

1956   makes national television debut on "Stage Show"; performs "Hound Dog" on "The Milton Berle Show," causing a national controversy; a record number of American television viewers watch Presley's first performance on "The Ed Sullivan Show"; *Love Me Tender,* Presley's first film, is released; "Heartbreak Hotel," "Don't Be Cruel," and "Love Me Tender" become hit records

1957   makes third and final appearance on "The Ed Sullivan Show," in which cameras only show Presley performing from the waist up; buys Graceland mansion in Memphis

1958   inducted into the Army

1960   discharged from Army; performs on "The Frank Sinatra Timex Special"

1966   wins Grammy for gospel album *How Great Thou Art*

1967   marries Priscilla Beaulieu in Las Vegas

1968   daughter Lisa Marie born; *Singer Presents Elvis (The '68 Comeback Special)* airs on NBC

1969   opens first of a series of sell-out concerts at the International Hotel in Las Vegas

1972   wins Grammy for gospel album *He Touched Me;* "Burning Love," Presley's last Top-Ten single, is released

1973   *Elvis: Aloha from Hawaii* is broadcast via satellite to several Asian countries, the first time a commercial television satellite special is broadcast over such a large area; divorces Priscilla Presley

1974   wins Grammy for gospel song "How Great Thou Art"

1977   dies at Graceland on August 16

Elvis Presley (1935–1977)

Many people around the world know that Elvis Presley was a famous singer and American icon, but few fully understand the scope of his contribution to popular music, which continues to earn him widespread acclaim. Presley combined different types of music to fashion a style called rockabilly, which became one of the key forms of rock 'n' roll. He fused the country-western music of the South with the rhythm and blues of African Americans and the popular music that dominated the radio and recording industries to create his own musical style. Presley was not the first to sing in a rock 'n' roll style, but his version of this new music became widely popular during the mid-1950's. He spread rock 'n' roll music across the country—and the world—taking it to a wide audience, especially teen-agers.

During the 1950's, American teen-agers had begun to think of themselves as being different from their parents' generation. For the

During the mid-1950's, Elvis Presley spread rock 'n' roll music across the country—and the world—taking it to a wide audience, especially teen-agers, who loved his style as well as his music.

first time in American history, teens had disposable income to spend on themselves. They dressed in styles of clothing that differed from that of adults; they went to movies that featured stars of their generation; and they listened to music that appealed to them. Presley's rock 'n' roll music, his hairstyle, and his fashion sense became a part of this new culture for teen-agers that was different from that of older generations.

Throughout his career, Presley changed his musical style and his personal look to keep up with the times and to gain popularity among older audiences. He became a movie star during the 1960's and then returned to live performances during the 1970's. Because his career went through many changes, he was popular with different types of people for different reasons. Even after his death, his popularity remains strong among a wide variety of people. This, plus his important role in American musical history, makes him a true legend.

Chapter 1: Early Life: From Tupelo to Memphis

In the early morning hours of Jan. 8, 1935, Elvis Aron Presley was born in East Tupelo, Mississippi, a small town nestled among the corn and cotton fields in the northern part of the state. The birth of Presley was both a happy and sad moment for his parents, Vernon and Gladys Presley. Thirty-five minutes earlier, his twin brother, Jessie Garon, had arrived into the world, but he was stillborn. The death of Jessie Garon ultimately had a deep impact on the Presley family. Presley was at times haunted by the loss of his twin, who would have been his only sibling, while Gladys kept her remaining son close to her. Presley and his mother would maintain an unusually tight bond throughout her short life.

The Presleys lived in a two-room house on Old Saltillo Road, which was in the poorest section of this small, rural town. The home was a type of dwelling known as a "shotgun shack" because it was so small and simply designed that if someone fired a shotgun into the house from the front, the bullet would fly out the back without going through any walls. Vernon Presley worked as a laborer in Tupelo, doing anything from driving a delivery truck to *sharecropping* (farming land for the owner in return for part of the crops). Gladys worked in a garment factory until about the time that Presley was born. Times were difficult for the small family, but they became worse in November 1937, when Vernon and two other men were arrested and charged with check forgery. Though the forged amount was small, the three men were given a harsh three-year sentence at Parchman Farm (Mississippi State Penitentiary), a prison farm where the inmates worked the land while serving their time.

Mrs. Presley was unable to keep up the payments on their house by herself, and she lost the house. She and her son stayed with various relatives until Vernon was released from prison early in February 1939. Vernon returned to working odd jobs, but the little family had a difficult time making enough money. As Mr. Presley moved from one job to another, he moved his family around Tupelo and East Tupelo from one rented home to another.

Elvis Presley, center, and his parents, Gladys and Vernon Presley, were a tightknit little family. Presley was born in Tupelo, Mississippi. The family moved to Memphis when Presley was a teen-ager.

Presley and his family may have been poor, but he had a secure childhood. There was always food on the table and clothes to wear. Also, the young boy knew that he was loved. He was not only close to his mother and father but also to his large extended family of aunts and uncles who helped each other during troubled times. His mother was devoted to his care and security, watching him carefully to keep him out of trouble and safe from harm.

The Presleys belonged to the First Assembly of God Church, where Mrs. Presley's uncle, Gains Mansell, was the preacher. In addition to providing moral guidance, the church gave the family a social life, while the gospel music sung by the congregation became a key musical influence on Presley. Gladys and Vernon sang in the church choir as did Presley when he grew old enough. Presley would sing gospel music for the rest of his life, not only among friends and family but also professionally. He recorded several albums of gospel music, and during the 1970's he often used a gospel quartet as back-up for his concerts on stage.

It is not known exactly when Presley became interested in playing music. He learned to play the guitar from his uncles and neighbors, particularly his uncle Vester Presley. Vester knew how to play more than gospel music, because he occasionally sang in Tupelo's honky-tonks, which were small, rough-and-tumble bars that hired local talent to attract customers. Elvis also entered the county fair talent contest one year at the insistence of his teacher, who had heard him sing in class. Each year on Children's Day, the Mississippi-Alabama Fair and Dairy Show sponsored an amateur talent contest, which was broadcast over Tupelo radio station WELO. The boy was quite young when he sang the ballad "Old Shep" for the talent show. He was so small that he had to stand on a chair to reach the microphone, and he sang with no musical accompaniment.

Not long after his experience at the fair, Presley began to express his interest in music. Local country singer Mississippi Slim, who hosted a couple of radio programs on WELO, became an important influence at this point. He taught the eager boy more chords on the guitar and may have provided him with an opportunity to play before an audience. The "WELO Jamboree" was an amateur hour hosted by Slim every Saturday afternoon. Presley hung around the radio station at every opportunity. Slim's real name was Carvel Lee Ausborn, and he was the brother of one of Presley's friends, James Ausborn. Through James, Presley had easy access to the entertainer, and he soaked up Slim's tales of being on the road and singing professionally. By the time he was in the seventh grade, Presley had begun taking his guitar to school on a regular basis. He would sing or play informally during the lunch hour, sometimes with another boy and sometimes alone.

By the fall of 1948, Tupelo had become a dead end for the Presleys. Work for Vernon was scarce, and the family decided to move to Memphis for better job opportunities, not unlike other rural families who left their farms and small towns after World War II (1939–1945) for the big cities. Later, Presley recalled, "We were broke, man, broke, and we left Tupelo overnight. Dad packed all our belongings in boxes and put them in the trunk and on top of a 1939 Plymouth. We just headed for Memphis. Things had to be better."[1]

MEMPHIS

The family's situation did improve in Memphis, with Vernon landing a job at a paint factory. Eventually, the Presleys moved into a housing project called the Lauderdale Courts, and Presley attended L.C. Humes High School. While the Courts were designed for families living at poverty level, they were not slums. A thriving, bustling atmosphere surrounded the Courts, and most of the residents worked hard to improve their lives. After a time, Presley's grandmother, Minnie Mae Presley, came from Tupelo to live with her son Vernon, and she remained a fixture in the Presley family for the rest of Presley's life. At one point, when Vernon and Gladys were both working, the Presleys' income exceeded the amount allowed by the Memphis Housing Authority for public housing recipients. The family had to move, but they chose to remain in the Lauderdale Courts neighborhood.

When Presley grew old enough, he also worked to help support the family and to earn his own spending money. At about this time, he began to look and dress a bit differently from the other teen-agers in his class. He grew his hair longer than the norm, and he used hair tonic to slick it back. He also grew sideburns, and he wore flashy clothes that he had purchased along Beale Street, an African American district where the "hip" musicians hung out. Occasionally, he brought his guitar to Humes to sing at school functions, but often he declined at the last minute, because he was too nervous to sing for his classmates. When he was a senior, he did perform in at least one talent show. However, his interest in music seemed to reveal itself more through what he was listening to than what he was playing.

The diversity of music on the Memphis radio stations was a reflection of the city's reputation as a crossroads for different types of music. On these local stations, Presley heard the different sounds and styles that would later influence him. WMPS played country-western music, as did WHHM, which featured local disc jockey favorite Sleepy-Eyed John. Big-band music was broadcast from high atop the landmark Peabody Hotel, while *rhythm and blues* (blues-based rock 'n' roll, also called r & b) artists were played on WDIA and WHBQ. African American disc jockeys staffed WDIA, and they showcased the music of Memphis's own blues and r & b musicians. WHBQ was best known for its most colorful disc jockey, Dewey Phillips, whose "Red Hot and Blue" program also favored blues and rhythm and blues.

In the 1950's, Memphis became the center of harmony-style gospel music. The top white gospel groups of the era performed at the "All-Night Gospel Sings" at Ellis Auditorium. Presley loved to attend the performances whenever possible. Though these shows featured a variety of gospel styles, it was the tight harmonies of the gospel quartets that attracted Presley the most. He was personally acquainted with the Blackwood Brothers, a quartet of brothers who attended the same Assembly of God church as the Presleys. But his favorite group was Hovie Lister and the Statesmen. The group dressed flamboyantly for a gospel quartet. Their singing style was highly emotional, and their performing style was exciting and energetic. They moved with the music.

Beale Street was home to the seedy clubs and rough joints where African American blues musicians had developed the r & b sound. Presley visited these clubs on occasion, and he bought his colorful shirts and slacks at Lansky Brothers on Beale, which was where many r & b musicians bought their clothes. Given Presley's young age, it is unlikely that he spent a lot of time in the clubs on Beale Street. But he could listen to blues and r & b at record shops, such as Poplar Tunes and Charlie's, where teen-agers could try out new records before buying them or play them on the jukebox.

At home, the Presleys listened to country-western music, and Presley was known to occasionally attend broadcasts of live entertainment at WMPS. Country music had undergone many changes during the 1940's that had permanently altered its sound and styles. For example, American country musician star Ernest Tubb featured the electric guitar on the "Grand Ole Opry," country music's most famous radio program. Also, western swing music, which developed in Texas and Oklahoma, combined country music with elements of big band jazz—including boogie-woogie—a jazz piano style that uses traditional blues chords and fast, exciting tempos—to form a contemporary sound that appealed to young audiences.

During his adolescence in Memphis, Presley listened to and appreciated all of these musical styles, absorbing them and learning from them. Not long after he graduated from high school, he was ready to test his musical talent, though it is unlikely he was planning a career in music.

SUN RECORDS

After graduating in the summer of 1953, Presley got a job at at M. B. Parker Machinists' Shop as a part-time helper in their small engine repair department. Soon after, he got a job on an ammunitions shell assembly line at Precision Tool. One Saturday afternoon, Presley walked into the Memphis Recording Service and told the woman behind the desk, Marion Keisker, that he wanted to cut a record. In the days before tape recorders were readily available to the mainstream public, recording services existed where people could record on an acetate disc (that is, a record) for a small fee. Presley recorded the song "My Happiness," a 1948 ballad that had been made famous by the Ink Spots, a popular African American vocal group, on a disc for a fee of $4 (about $29 today).

The recording service was owned by Sam Phillips, who also owned Sun Records, an independent record label in Memphis which had been recording r & b artists since 1950. Phillips enjoyed a national reputation for discovering talented r & b singers. He paid the musicians, financed the sessions, and recorded the artists himself in his little studio on Union Avenue. He generally leased the master recordings to various small record companies across the country, who then released the songs on their own labels. Phillips was always looking for new talent and, more than likely, Presley was hoping to catch his attention when he walked into the studio that day. Unfortunately, the producer was not there at the time, and Keisker was running the service alone. She noticed Presley's long, slicked-back hair and sideburns and asked him what kind of music he sang and whom he sounded like. He answered, "I don't sound like nobody,"[2] which made her curious, so she taped the young singer on the studio's master tape recorder while he made his disc. After "My Happiness," Presley recorded another Ink Spots song, "That's When Your Heartaches Begin," to go on the other side.

Phillips had told Keisker that rhythm and blues could become popular with the general public if he could find a white performer who could sing with the sound and feel of a black performer. Because Presley chose two songs made famous by the Ink Spots, Keisker thought that Sam Phillips might be interested in the polite young man. But when the producer finally listened to the two recordings, he thought the young man was an "interesting"[3] singer but that he needed a lot of work.

Presley returned to the Memphis Recording Service in January 1954 to record two more songs, "Casual Love Affair" and a country-western song "I'll Never Stand in Your Way." This time, Phillips worked the controls. The producer took down the young singer's name and address, but he did not offer him much encouragement. Around this time, Presley took a job delivering supplies for Crown Electric Company, and had begun to think of becoming an electrician.

In June 1954, Sam Phillips finally called Presley. The producer thought that the young singer might be a good fit for a ballad he wanted recorded called "Without You." Presley rushed down to the tiny Sun studio and gave the song his best effort. However, he could not seem to capture whatever Phillips wanted for the song, so Sam had him run through every tune that he knew. Phillips thought that Presley needed practice and seasoning, so he suggested to Scotty Moore, a guitar player with the Starlite Wranglers, that he, Presley, and bass player Bill Black should get together.

Sam Phillips, right foreground, *owner of Sun Records in Memphis, helped give Presley his start when he recorded him in 1954. Presley is shown in the background,* left, *with bass player Bill Black,* center, *and guitarist Scotty Moore. The trio had a local hit in Memphis with "That's All Right."*

In early July, the trio began work in Sun's studio. One evening, after trying a few ballads that yielded nothing special, the group finally hit on something while improvising during a break. Presley started singing Arthur "Big Boy" Crudup's old blues song "That's All Right" with a fast rhythm and a casual style. Moore and Black quickly picked up their instruments and joined in. Phillips was excited by the trio's fresh sound, and he eagerly recorded it. A few nights later, they recorded their version of Bill Monroe's country bluegrass hit "Blue Moon of Kentucky." The two songs became the group's first single release, which is a record with one song on each side. That first record—with a blues tune on one side and a country classic on the other—clearly shows the roots of Presley's music.

Presley's versions of both songs were stylistically unlike the originals. His approach was more easygoing, giving his interpretations an air of spontaneity. He replaced the hard vocal delivery and slow rhythm of Crudup's version of "That's All Right" with a relaxed vocal style and fast pace. Likewise for "Blue Moon of Kentucky," the tempo was increased, and two elements were added that would make Presley famous—syncopation and reverberation. Presley's syncopation of certain lyrics gave them a hiccuplike effect as he sang, while the reverberation during recording created a slight echo. Presley's style became known as rockabilly, which referred to the mix of country music, commonly called "hillbilly," with r & b that has been relaxed and speeded up, or "rocked."

Sam Phillips knew he had something special in "That's All Right" and "Blue Moon of Kentucky." He personally delivered a copy of "That's All Right" to the hottest disc jockey in Memphis, Dewey Phillips (no relation). Dewey hesitated to spin the record on his WHBQ program "Red Hot and Blue," because he preferred to play the r & b music of African American artists. But, the disc jockey truly liked what he heard. When he introduced "That's All Right" on his program, phone and telegram requests poured in for the deejay to play it again. Dewey played the song over and over until he decided to put the unknown singer on his program that very night.

While his record was making its radio debut, Presley was trying to relax at the movies. Dewey Phillips phoned the Presley home and asked for Presley to come to the radio station for an interview. Presley's parents dashed to the Suzore No. 2 theater to retrieve Presley. Vernon and Gladys went up and down the aisles of the theater until they found their son, then raced with him to the radio station. Phillips told the nervous young singer he would alert him when they would be on the air. He asked Presley several questions about his life and interests, trying to put him at ease. Phillips then thanked his guest for his time. Presley asked if Phillips was going to interview him on air. Phillips replied, "I already have. The mike's been open the whole time."[4] According to Phillips, Presley broke out in a cold sweat.

After the buzz created by the "Red Hot and Blue" program, Sam Phillips sent "That's All Right" and "Blue Moon of Kentucky" to the factory to be pressed as both a 78-rpm single and a 45-rpm single. The phenomenal career of Elvis Presley was launched.

Chapter 2: Early Career:
From the Hillbilly Cat to Soldier Boy

Thanks in part to Dewey Phillips's enthusiasm for Presley, "That's All Right" created a stir in Memphis, selling 6,300 copies in three weeks. The record climbed to number three on the local country-western charts, eventually selling 30,000 copies across the South. On July 30, 1954, Presley made his first public appearance, at the Overton Park Shell in Memphis. Accompanied by Scotty Moore and Bill Black, Presley was one of several acts on the program that evening. The headliner was country yodeler Slim Whitman. Elvis Presley was so unknown to the music scene that he was billed as "Ellis Presley" in some of the ads for the event.

Like a tightly wound spring, the young singer moved all over the stage as he performed his two songs. He may have had a touch of stage fright given the circumstances, but the young man had always been full of nervous energy. Performing live gave him an outlet for the release of his pent-up energy. He continually shook his leg while he sang, and some of the teen-agers in the audience screamed, apparently in response to the movement. Backstage, he asked Moore why the audience had been screaming. Somewhat surprised at the audience reaction himself, the guitarist remarked that he thought it was the way Presley was shaking his leg. Much later, Presley's on-stage movements would become controversial, making the singer infamous as well as famous.

After the Overton performance, the trio began to sing at tiny clubs around Memphis, such as the Eagle's Nest, the Bel Air, and the Airport Inn. They also performed at the opening of a shopping center, using the back of a flatbed truck as a stage. Though audiences could hear that Presley's style was not the same as typical country-western music or r & b, no one quite knew how to describe it. The terms "rockabilly" and "rock 'n' roll" were not yet commonly used. As he became known in the Memphis area, local journalists called his music "rural rhythm," or they referred to Presley as having "a white man's voice singing negro rhythms with a rural flavor."[1]

Despite having a unique style influenced by blues and r & b, Presley was still listed under the country-western category, or "hillbilly music" as it was called then. When he toured, he did so with country performers on the country music circuits across the South. When his songs made the charts, they appeared on the country-western charts. As long as he was labeled a country performer, there was little controversy about his music or performing style.

Phillips released another record by Presley, Moore, and Black at the end of September 1954. It had an r & b tune called "Good Rockin' Tonight" on one side and a country tune, "I Don't Care if the Sun Don't Shine," on the other. The following year, Sun Records released three more singles by Presley and his band. They included "Milkcow Blues Boogie" backed by "You're a Heartbreaker," "Baby Let's Play House" backed by "I'm Left, You're Right, She's Gone," and "Mystery Train" backed by "I Forgot to Remember to Forget." Each record followed the same pattern, with a blues or r & b song featured on one side, and a country-western song on the other. The selection of songs was much like Presley's musical style, because it represented a combination of types of music.

THE GRAND OLE OPRY AND THE LOUISIANA HAYRIDE

On the strength of their first two records, Presley, Scotty, and Bill, who came to be known as the Hillbilly Cat and the Blue Moon Boys, appeared live on the "Grand Ole Opry" on Oct. 2, 1954. On the "Opry," popular performers sang live in front of a large audience, and the program was broadcast across the South every Saturday night by Nashville radio station WSM. The "Opry" was—and still is—devoted to the most traditional style of country music. So, it was not surprising that Presley and his accelerated music were not well received by the audience or Opry management. The young singer was devastated by the negative reaction because, like most rural Southerners, he and his family had been fans of the "Opry" much of their lives.

Less than two weeks later, the Hillbilly Cat and the Blue Moon

Boys were hired to appear on the "Louisiana Hayride," which was another radio show that broadcast live performances in front of an audience. However, the "Hayride," which was broadcast from Shreveport, Louisiana, was dedicated to showcasing new styles of country music and attracted a younger audience than the "Opry." The Hillbilly Cat and the Blue Moon Boys fit right in at the "Hayride." The band continued to perform there until Presley became too famous to play such a small venue. The Blue Moon Boys picked up a new band member

from the "Hayride." D. J. Fontana, who played drums regularly on the show, decided to quit the "Hayride" in early 1955 and cast his fate with Presley.

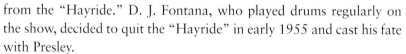

After his success on the "Louisiana Hayride," Presley felt secure enough to quit his day job. In October 1954, he left Crown Electric. The following month, the band set up an informal arrangement with Bob Neal to book their shows. Neal was a disc jockey for country radio station WMPS, and he had many connections in the local music business. Neal was formally contracted at the start of 1955. As manager of the Hillbilly Cat and the Blue Moon Boys, Neal pushed the group's records, booked tours across the South with big-name country acts, and handled all their business arrangements.

By this time, Presley had fine-tuned his performing style, in which he moved his hips, shook his legs, and sometimes fell to the floor. He was influenced by the flamboyant movements of the gospel quartets, the deep feeling of the blues performers, and the rhythm behind the r & b singers. He combined them all into a unique performing style, which he used to work the audiences into a frenzy. In addition, Bill Black often danced and rolled around on the floor with his huge bass fiddle. The group's performances were sometimes considered too wild in small towns, and a few country singers did not like to

Presley performed with Black and Moore as the Hillbilly Cat and the Blue Moon Boys on the Louisiana Hayride radio show in Shreveport. The group performed on the show beginning in 1954 until Presley became too famous to play such a small venue.

perform after Presley, because the crowd was too worked up after his act. However, in larger towns, they were a hit, and it was not long before Presley attracted the attention of a man who would change his life, Colonel Tom Parker.

THE COLONEL

In the spring of 1955, the Hillbilly Cat and the Blue Moon Boys were booked on a couple of tours with country-western singer Hank Snow. The tours were controlled by Snow's company, Jamboree Attractions, which was managed by Colonel Tom Parker, a former carnival worker. Parker was not called "colonel" because he had been in the army. Instead, "colonel" was an honorary title given to him by the state of Louisiana. It was an old custom in the South to award the title to people who had done a service or brought acclaim to a Southern state. Parker used his carnival connections to get the title from the state's governor. Throughout his life, Parker liked to be called the Colonel. Most people obliged, whether they liked the cantankerous manager, or not. Parker noticed the kind of popularity that Presley had among teen-age girls when he performed. He believed that Presley could become a major star, not just in the South but across the whole country.

In August 1955, Presley signed a special contract with Parker, even though he was still under contract with Bob Neal. Parker wanted to get started on his plan to make Presley a national star, so Neal stepped back to let Parker manage Presley and the band. When Neal's contract expired in March 1956, Parker became Presley's sole manager, and Presley became Parker's only client.

Parker was the motivating force behind Presley becoming an internationally famous singing star. He negotiated to get Presley a recording contract with RCA, a large, national recording company. Sam Phillips willingly sold Presley's recording contract to RCA in the fall of 1955. Sun

Colonel Tom Parker, left, became Presley's manager in 1955. Parker was the motivating force behind Presley's superstardom.

Records was too small to launch a national recording artist, and Phillips was more interested in exploring local talent, so he was satisfied with the deal. The money that Phillips got was supposedly the most ever paid for a contract release for a country-western artist.

However, Parker and RCA executives decided to stop promoting Presley as strictly a country-western performer. Instead, they would promote him on all three national charts—country-western, pop, and r & b. Fans of pop music came from all over the country, while fans of country music tended to be in the South. Promoting Presley as a pop singer would expose him to other parts of the country and increase his fan base. As odd as it might seem now, Parker did not even consider promoting Presley as a rock 'n' roll singer. Though rock 'n' roll music had been around for a few years, it was not considered a major genre, or style, of music. There were no rock 'n' roll charts—at least not yet.

"ELVIS THE PELVIS"

In January 1956, Presley recorded "Heartbreak Hotel," his first single for RCA. Unlike the songs he had recorded for Sun Records, this tune had been written especially for him. The lyrics, blueslike sound, and dramatic tone of the song were crafted to fit his style of singing and performing. The song's tale of heartbreak and Presley's emotional delivery were designed to attract teen-agers, who were becoming his biggest fans. "Heartbreak Hotel" quickly made the Top Ten on the pop, country-western, and r & b charts—just as Colonel Parker and RCA had planned. By late fall of 1956, four more Presley songs accomplished the same feat: "I Want You, I Need You, I Love You," "Don't Be Cruel," "Hound Dog," and "Love Me Tender." That year, there was enough material to release his first album, which was titled *Elvis Presley*. Another of Parker's ideas was to promote Presley as an individual singer instead of the front man for a group. After he signed with RCA, the Blue Moon Boys were not mentioned on record labels or in publicity.

Throughout 1956, Presley recorded music that moved away from the pure rockabilly of his Sun recordings. The "hiccupping" of the lyrics and the echo effect that had defined his Sun sound gave way to a smooth, more polished rock 'n' roll style. Instead of the rough edges of "Good Rockin' Tonight," for example, Presley preferred the smoothness of "Don't Be Cruel," one of his biggest hits of the year. This fine-tuning of his musical style helped win legions of young fans and helped make rock 'n' roll a popular genre in the mid-1950's.

The most successful part of Parker's plan to make Presley a national star was the decision to put him on television. Commercial television had not been widely developed until after World War II (1939–1945). It did not become popular with the public until the early 1950's, when coast-to-coast broadcasting became possible. That meant that a program airing on the East Coast could be picked up and viewed on the West Coast at the same time. Throughout the 1950's, TV became increasingly popular, until it surpassed the movies as America's number-one form of entertainment. It could be said that Presley's career and the popularity of television took off at about the same time. However, even Parker could not have anticipated what would happen to Presley over the next year.

Presley signed a contract to appear four times on a television program called "Stage Show"—although he would actually appear on the show six times. The program was a family-oriented variety show, in which several different singers, dancers, and comedians performed in front of a live studio audience in New York City. It was hosted by two musicians who had been popular in the 1940's, Tommy and Jimmy Dorsey. On Jan. 28, 1956, Presley made his national television debut on "Stage Show."

The other performers on that evening's show seemed tame in comparison to Presley. Sarah Vaughan, a well-known jazz singer, appeared in an evening gown and sang in an established style, and a banjo-playing comedian performed his routine.

When it was Presley's turn, he exploded onto the stage as if he had been shot out of a cannon. While he sang "Shake, Rattle, and Roll"— segueing into "Flip, Flop and Fly"—and "I Got a Woman," he moved his body constantly. During the instrumental break in each song, he stood back and shook his entire body to the beat of the music. A few girls in the audience screamed, which made the singer smile. Compared to the smooth, polished performances of the other guests,

Presley seemed wild and dangerous. In addition, his long, slicked-back hair came tumbling down on his face when he moved, and his Beale Street clothes looked exotic. He was signed to do two more appearances because the reaction to his performance was so strong.

Presley improved his performances each time he appeared on "Stage Show." By the last two shows in March, he had become experienced at getting the studio audience worked up when he sang. He dramatically strummed the opening chords to songs and then paused, waiting for the girls to scream. He moved freely and loosely throughout the performance, and he made eye contact with the camera and the studio audience. He swung or gyrated his hips and rolled his leg, which also made the girls scream. With each Presley appearance, "Stage Show" received higher and higher ratings. He soon became a much sought-after television guest.

Parker made few mistakes in guiding Presley's career. But he did make an error in judgement in April 1956 when he booked the young singer into the New Frontier, a big Las Vegas hotel and nightclub. At that time, Las Vegas was an adult vacation spot, and the clubs preferred to book the big pop and jazz performers of the period, such as Frank Sinatra, Rosemary Clooney, and Louis Prima. The adult audiences at the New Frontier did not understand Presley's Southern-based rockabilly. After a few performances, he was bumped to being the second act.

Also in April, an article about Presley and his sudden celebrity appeared in *Life*, a national magazine which was famous for its photos. The article, titled "A Howling Hillbilly Success," painted a disapproving picture of Presley and his fans. It mentioned an event in Texas in which young fans broke through a glass door trying to get to Presley so he could autograph parts of their bodies. It also showed photos of Presley in concert with his fans storming the stage. Those who did not know Presley and his music might think that he was a dangerous influence on teen-agers. Over the next few weeks, articles in *Time, Newsweek, Look*, and other magazines reinforced this idea by focusing on the way he excited his teen-age audiences with his music and his hip-swiveling performance style. In addition, some articles made fun of his clothing and hairstyle, while others suggested his rural Southern accent was an indication that he was ignorant. Some articles even claimed he had been in and out of jail, sold drugs, and was dying of leukemia—all of which were, of course, untrue—and Parker set the record straight immediately.

These articles appeared at the same time that rock 'n' roll music in general was being criticized by the press and by the public. Just as Presley was becoming a household name, *Time, Life, Newsweek*, and other magazines and newspapers were printing articles about the dangers of rock 'n' roll music. The articles jumped to conclusions by associating the new music with a rise in the rate of juvenile crime. Parker's plans for promoting Presley in the pop music market were thwarted by the bad publicity surrounding Presley and rock 'n' roll. The singer did not become associated with the mainstream pop-music industry as Parker had wanted. Instead, he became known as a notorious rock 'n' roller. The press gave him several nicknames to suggest this image, including "Elvis the Pelvis," a name Presley despised.

The rumors, criticism, and bad publicity snowballed into a full-blown controversy on June 5, 1956, when Presley made his second appearance on "The Milton Berle Show." The Berle program was a variety show similar to "Stage Show" in that it featured a number of entertainers who performed their latest songs, dances, or comedy routines in individual segments. But "The Milton Berle Show" was one of the most popular programs of the 1950's, and it had a higher profile among the viewers and the media. That evening, Presley sang "Hound Dog" for the first time on television. He had heard the song performed by another singer during his disastrous Las Vegas engagement and decided to include a version of it in his act. Since he had not recorded it yet, no one knew what to expect. As he sang the first verses, the live audience in the television studio responded well. This encouraged Presley to push his performance further. He slowed down the final chorus to a blues tempo, and then he thrust his hips to the hard-driving beat. The studio audience screamed with excitement.

The next day, journalists expressed outrage over Presley's provocative performance. They felt that he had gone too far. Many compared his performing style to a striptease. A reviewer for the

New York Herald Tribune named John Crosby summed up what many believed when he called Presley "unspeakably untalented and vulgar."[2] Presley's performance on the Berle show gave the people who were critical of rock 'n' roll a specific example to rally around. Parents, the media, religious groups, and even the PTA (Parent-Teacher Association) expressed concern about the negative influence of this type of music.

Despite the criticism, other television producers were eager to have Presley on their shows. The controversy attracted viewers and increased the ratings. A month after "The Milton Berle Show," Presley appeared on "The Steve Allen Show," a variety series that focused on comedy skits. The Allen program had just premiered in June, and it was on at the same time as "The Ed Sullivan Show." Sullivan's program was considered the high point of variety programs, and Steve Allen was determined to give Sullivan a run for his money. In the days before cable and syndicated television stations, competition for viewers among the networks was fierce. Allen knew that Presley was a good choice to lure viewers away from the Sullivan program.

Allen wanted Presley, but he did not want the criticism. Instead of having the hot, young entertainer perform in his usual style, he asked Presley to sing "Hound Dog" to a real basset hound. The dog, wearing a top hat, sat on a pedestal while Presley stood next to him in a tuxedo. The singer held the dog's long face in his hands, and then belted out the song. The studio audience giggled, the viewers at home got a glimpse of Presley's sense of humor, and the TV critics had less to complain about. Elvis the Pelvis had been tamed—at least temporarily.

Presley's sexy dance moves caused controversy early in his career. He was shown from only the waist up when he made his last appearance on "The Ed Sullivan Show" on Jan. 8, 1957, shown above.

"A REAL DECENT, FINE BOY"

"The Steve Allen Show" beat "The Ed Sullivan Show" by a wide margin in the ratings that evening, which was a major feat in the 1950's television wars. After those ratings were reported in the newspapers, Sullivan became the last variety-show host to ask Presley to appear on his program.

Sullivan, who had established his reputation as a savvy show-biz columnist for a major New York newspaper, was a powerful figure in the television industry. An appearance on his show meant an act or entertainer had made the big time. It was the seal of approval in mainstream show business. Parker had tried to get Presley on the Sullivan show earlier that year, but Sullivan did not want to pay Parker's asking price of $5,000 (about $36,000 today) for his client. Sullivan then publicly declared that he would not allow Presley on his show, because he was not "his cup of tea." This was an obvious reference and criticism of Presley's sexy, hip-swiveling performing style. But ratings speak louder than personal taste and, after the Allen show, Sullivan changed his mind. He wanted the good ratings that booking Presley would bring, but Sullivan also knew that if he did not have Presley on his show, his program's reputation as a showcase for the latest talent might suffer. Parker signed Presley to appear on "The Ed Sullivan Show" for an unprecedented fee of $50,000 (about $360,000 today) for three performances. It was a much higher fee than if Sullivan had signed him earlier.

Presley appeared on the Sullivan show on Sept. 9 and Oct. 28, 1956, and on Jan. 8, 1957. In his first appearance, he introduced the title song from his first film, *Love Me Tender* (1956). He also sang "Don't Be Cruel," "Ready Teddy," and a shortened version of "Hound Dog." He moved freely around the stage, and the girls in the studio audience screamed, though the camera sometimes cut away from Presley to show his new backup singers, the Jordanaires. For the October appearance, he sang the same songs, except he replaced "Ready Teddy" with the ballad "Love Me." Again, he teased the studio audience with his performing style, smiling into the camera every time he made the girls shriek.

For his last appearance, Presley sang a medley of his biggest hits and a couple of new tunes. He concluded with a gospel song, "Peace in the Valley," which he dedicated to Hungarian refugees and other victims of the Soviet invasion of Hungary in November 1956. Afterward, Sullivan declared on camera to the whole television viewing audience that Presley was "a real decent, fine boy" and "a very nice person." The statement was considered a validation of Presley by Sullivan, and the singer appreciated the gesture. The surprising part of this final show was that the network censors at CBS decided that the cameras should film Presley only from the waist up. It was odd that they decided to do this for his third appearance but not for his first two. However, the incident has become part of the Presley legend. It is often used to explain how controversial the singer was in 1956. As for Presley, he once explained his "controversial" movements simply: "Rock and roll music, if you like it and if you feel it, you can't help but move to it. That's what happens to me. I can't help it."[3]

In addition to these television appearances throughout 1956 and early 1957, Presley continued to tour around the country. Controversy often accompanied him, even in the South, where he had been touring since 1954. In August 1956, a judge in Jacksonville, Florida, ordered him not to shake his legs and gyrate (that is, swivel) his hips. He obliged, but when he wiggled his little finger on stage during "Hound Dog," the girls in the audience shrieked anyway. Presley had appeared in Florida in 1955, shaking his legs and swinging his hips in his usual style. But he had been billed as a country singer back then. In 1956, when he was called a rock 'n' roller, that same performance style was suddenly considered provocative and dangerous. The reputation that rock 'n' roll and Presley had earned by 1956 was much worse than the actual music or performances. It was a pattern that would be repeated in later years when other controversial performers burst onto the music scene.

Parker fought Presley's negative image and reputation with his own tactics. The on-air endorsement of his client by Ed Sullivan helped balance the bad publicity. But Parker also made sure that Presley was photographed donating to charities. He also allowed high-school students to interview Presley for their school newspapers. And, he treated the fan clubs well, offering them trinkets and inside information. Presley was genuinely grateful to his fans. He never hesitated to sign an autograph or pose for a photo. When local fans showed up at his home in Memphis, he often personally greeted them, and his mother sometimes made them ice tea and lemonade. This helped create a very loyal fan base for Presley, and it showed another side to his personality.

ELVIS THE MOVIE STAR

On a much larger scale, the one aspect of Presley's career that truly aided in overcoming his image as a dangerous rock 'n' roller was his starring roles in several Hollywood films. Between 1956 and 1958, Presley appeared in four films. Three of them were very loosely based on Presley's life and career, though they told fictional stories. The films helped older audiences accept him and his music.

In April 1956, the singer signed a movie contract with legendary producer Hal Wallis. Wallis had been a producer in the movie business since the 1930's. One of his most famous films was the classic *Casablanca* (1942). During the 1950's, he had discovered several entertainers who would become big stars, including Dean Martin, Jerry Lewis, and Shirley McLaine. Presley had been an avid moviegoer as a teen-ager and he had aspirations to become a movie actor. He once said, "Singers come and go, but if you're a good actor, you can last a long time."[4]

Wallis made his movies for Paramount Pictures. When he first signed Presley, he did not have a script or project available for him. So, he loaned him out to Twentieth Century Fox. There, Presley co-starred in the Civil War drama *Love Me Tender*. Presley played a secondary role in the film as Clint Reno, the youngest brother of the main character, Vance (played by Richard Egan), and he got to sing four songs. The title song, "Love Me Tender," was an adaptation of an old Civil War ballad called "Aura Lee." Presley introduced the ballad on his first Ed Sullivan appearance, which helped to promote the movie and make the song one of his biggest hits.

In a dance sequence choreographed especially for him, Presley had the opportunity to show off his moves while performing the title song in the movie Jailhouse Rock *(1957).*

Presley got along well with his co-stars, and he tried to learn from their experience, especially from the star, Egan. Presley developed a crush on Debra Paget, the actress who played his wife in the film, but she was too concerned with her career to begin a romance. Still, the three of them—Egan, Paget, and Presley—became fast friends on the set.

The movie reviewers were brutal when *Love Me Tender* was released in November 1956. They harshly criticized Presley's acting. A reviewer for *Time* magazine even compared his acting and screen presence to that of a corpse, describing him as "smooth and damp-looking" like "a 172-pound sausage six feet tall."[5] The reviews did not matter, because the film was a box-office hit. When a huge wooden cut-out of Presley as Clint Reno was unveiled on top of a New York City theater to promote the film, thousands of fans showed up to see the larger-than-life Presley.

The first movie that Presley made for producer Hal Wallis was a musical drama called *Loving You* (released July 1957). It was developed and written by director Hal Kantor especially for Presley.

Kantor followed the singer around starting in December 1956 to get an idea of what his life as a popular entertainer was like. He then incorporated his observations and experiences into the script.

In the movie, Presley plays a singer named Deke Rivers. Deke comes from the South, but his singing and performing style does not conform to traditional country-western music. A ruthless music promoter recognizes Deke's talents and knows that his fresh, new sound will appeal to young audiences. In the story, the press misrepresents Deke as a hothead, and parents are afraid that his new music is a bad influence on their children. However, at the end, Deke proves that he is a nice boy who has been misunderstood, and that his music is not any more dangerous than the music of previous generations.

The comparisons between the fictional Deke Rivers and the real-life experiences of Presley are obvious. In the movie, there is a happy ending that explains that Deke and his music were really misunderstood. The filmmakers, Colonel Parker, and others connected with Presley's career were hoping that the public would believe that about Presley and his music, too.

Jailhouse Rock (released October 1957) and *King Creole* (released July 1958) were similar to *Loving You*, though not as closely based on Presley's life and career. In *Jailhouse Rock*, Presley plays Vince Everett, whose quick temper gets him into fistfights. When he accidentally causes the death of a man during a fight, he is sent to jail. In jail, he becomes bitter, but he learns to sing and play the guitar from an older prisoner. When he gets out of jail, he becomes a famous singer with a new sound that attracts the teen-agers. His manager, Peggy (Judy Tyler), understands the real Vince Everett, and she brings out his true personality because she loves him. In *King Creole*, Presley stars as Danny Fisher, who is from a poor family in New Orleans. Danny is angry at the world because his mother has died and his father cannot seem to get over her death. He has to work to help out the family because his father cannot hold a job. Danny gets involved with juvenile delinquents and gangsters as a way to make money quickly, but he learns that a better way to make a living is through his music. His unique style of singing becomes the new sensation of the French Quarter, a famous New Orleans district, and it attracts young fans to the club where he works.

Of the four movies Presley acted in during the 1950's, *King Creole* is perhaps the best. Besides Presley, it starred some fine actors of the period, including Walter Matthau, Carolyn Jones, Dean Jagger, Vic Morrow, Dolores Hart, and Paul Stewart. It was directed by Michael Curtiz, who had been working in Hollywood since the 1930's. He knew producer Hal Wallis very well, and he had directed *Casablanca* for Wallis in 1942. The songs that Presley sang in the film, such as "Trouble," "King Creole," and "Crawfish," were written by some of the best songwriters of the day. Mike Stoller and Jerry Leiber, who had written the song "Jailhouse Rock," wrote "Trouble" as a blues song in the style of such bluesmen as Muddy Waters. "Crawfish," which was written by Ben Weisman and Fred Wise, was a duet that Presley sang with r & b singer Kitty White. She played a street vendor selling crawfish in the French Quarter where Presley's character lives. She advertises her wares by singing about them, and Presley joins in as she passes by his house. The scene captures the flavor of New Orleans, where street vendors actually used to sell their wares in this way. The music that Presley sang in his films was a more polished version of the style he had been performing since the beginning of his career.

One of the most important aspects of *Loving You, Jailhouse Rock*, and *King Creole* was the type of character Presley played. In all three movies, Presley starred as a singer with a new sound who seems to be rough and dangerous on the surface. But, as the story unfolds, people discover that he is misunderstood, and that his music is worthwhile even if it sounds a bit different. The idea was that if Presley played this type of character on the big screen, then maybe audiences and the press would see him that way in real life. Becoming a movie star did help Presley become more accepted by the entertainment industry, even if some adults still found him controversial. He was very professional on the set, got along well with his co-stars, and listened closely to his producer and director.

By the end of 1956, Presley had become so famous that he had to move from the small house he had bought for his family earlier that year. In the spring of 1957, he purchased a small mansion on the outskirts of Memphis. The house had been named Graceland by the previous owners, and Presley and his family kept the name. Gladys Presley had seen the house first, and because she liked it so much, Presley bought it. Not long after, the famous Music Gates were added to the front to keep out unwanted fans and visitors. The wrought-iron gates feature two stylized figures of guitar players with musical notes bridging the space between them. Graceland would be Presley's primary home for the rest of his life. Unlike other celebrities and movie stars, he did not relocate to Hollywood or New York. He preferred to stay in Memphis, the city he called his hometown.

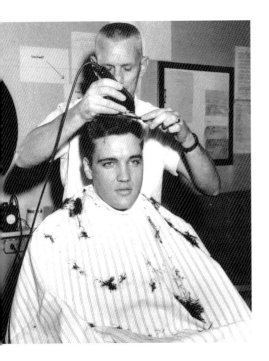

Presley was inducted into the Army in 1958. Although getting his famous locks shorn for his Army buzzcut was well publicized, Presley wanted to be treated like any other Army inductee.

Presley did not get to enjoy his new house for very long. At the end of 1957, he was drafted by the U.S. Army. He was able to get a postponement (called a deferment), so that he did not have to go immediately. This allowed him to finish *King Creole* before he was called up.

On March 24, 1958, Elvis Aron Presley was inducted into the U.S. Army. He was stationed in Fort Hood, Texas, for basic training. As an entertainer, Presley could have joined the Special Services of the Army. If he had, he would have traveled around the world to entertain American soldiers wherever they were stationed. This would have been an easier and safer tour of duty than that of the average soldier. However, he turned down the Army's offer to join Special Services, choosing to serve his country like any other American inductee.

On Aug. 14, 1958, five months after Presley entered the Army, Gladys Presley died in Memphis, possibly from complications related to hepatitis. Presley, who had always been close to his mother, was devastated by her death. He broke down many times in front of reporters, friends, and family in the days before her funeral. Gladys

Presley had loved her son very much, and she had been his biggest supporter. Her death was the worst event in his life up to that point, and in many ways, he never got over it.

After his mother's funeral, Presley was sent to Friedberg, in what was then West Germany, to serve out his two years of military service in the Third Armored Division. The only concession the Army made to his celebrity was to allow him to live off-base with his family in nearby Bad Nauheim, so that he could have a bit of privacy. Presley was also well known in Europe, and it was necessary to keep him from fans and reporters. Despite the precautions of the Army, the constant presence of fans and reporters made it difficult for him to do any sight-seeing when he was off duty.

Presley's father, Vernon, and his paternal grandmother, Minnie Mae, joined him shortly after he arrived in Germany. They were later joined by various friends and cousins, because Presley liked to be surrounded by family and friends. Toward the end of his tour of duty, Presley met a 14-year-old girl who impressed him very much. Priscilla Ann Beaulieu was the stepdaughter of an Air Force officer also stationed in Germany. Despite her young age, Presley and Priscilla dated frequently the last few weeks he was stationed in Germany, though they were seldom alone. Priscilla was at the airport to say good-bye when his tour of duty was over, and she was photographed waving to him and crying. When he returned to the States, reporters asked him about her, but he downplayed their relationship, probably to protect her and her family from the press.

While Presley was in the Army, some speculated that being away from the public for two years would hurt his career. However, he was not totally absent from the music scene. Parker and RCA made sure that he had recorded enough material so that a few singles could be released while he was in the Army. Also, *King Creole* was not released until after he was inducted, which helped keep him in the public eye.

Most importantly, Presley's tour of duty did much to improve his image with the public. If there was one event that changed the public's negative attitudes toward Presley, it was his willingness to serve his country, like any regular American soldier.

Chapter 3: The Rebel Grows Up

As soon as Sergeant Elvis Presley was discharged from the Army on March 5, 1960, RCA and Colonel Parker whisked him away to Nashville to cut a new album and some singles. He enjoyed only two weeks of restful civilian life before pushing forward with his career.

Parker chartered a bus to take Presley and a group of close friends to Nashville for Presley's first recording session in almost two years. Presley was joined by his old associates guitarist Scotty Moore and drummer D. J. Fontana. Bill Black, who had played stand-up bass for Presley, did not rejoin the band. Moore, Black, and Fontana had been Presley's backup musicians during most of his early career, though they had problems working for Parker. Parker did not want the band to take the limelight from Presley, and he did not pay them very well. This often created tension. When Presley entered the Army, Black took the opportunity to form his own group, Bill Black's Combo. In 1960, their recording "White Silver Sands" reached number nine on the pop singles chart and number one on the black singles chart. Black did not achieve the level of fame and recognition he had experienced with Presley, but he was happy making his own music. After Presley returned from the Army, Moore continued to record with Presley in the studio on a free-lance basis until 1968. Fontana, who had been recruited from the "Louisiana Hayride," had a different arrangement than either Moore or Black. That allowed him more freedom in his career. The Jordanaires, a gospel quartet, supported Presley on vocals. The quartet had begun singing backup for Presley in 1956, and they continued to do so until well into the 1960's. Presley's insistence on having the Jordanaires on his recordings shows how influential gospel music continued to be on the singer.

In addition to old pals Moore and Fontana, and the familiar faces of the Jordanaires, other musicians were hired for these sessions. The famed country-western pianist Floyd Cramer had signed on, offering his smooth piano stylings to the music.

During the overnight recording session, Presley cut the rock 'n' roll tune "Stuck on You," which became his first post-army single. A couple of weeks later, Presley returned to the RCA studio in Nashville to record the tracks needed to make an entire album. By the end of April, *Elvis Is Back* was released. In less than two months, RCA had cut and pressed a new Presley album, and it was playing on the radio nationwide.

Just as the musicians were a mix of the familiar and the new, so were the songs selected for the album. They included Presley's usual mix of rock 'n' roll, country, and r & b tunes, but a few of the numbers were more mellow and smooth, like pop music. One of the pop-styled songs was "Fever," which Peggy Lee had made famous two years earlier. Not all the songs that Presley recorded in April were included in the album. Two of his most famous ballads, "It's Now or Never" and "Are You Lonesome Tonight?" were held back for later release. These two songs were also influenced by pop music.

"Are You Lonesome Tonight?" was not like the music Presley had sung before he went into the Army. American singer Al Jolson had introduced this sad ballad in the 1920's, but Presley was probably more familiar with a 1959 version of the song that had been recorded by pop singer Jaye P. Morgan. Parker is believed to have urged Presley to record "Are You Lonesome Tonight?," though it was unusual for him to interfere with his client's choice of music. Despite its history as a pop song, "Are You Lonesome Tonight?" did well on the country music charts for Presley. He would not record another song that hit the country charts until 1968—a signal that his music was taking a different direction.

A unique feature of "Are You Lonesome Tonight?" is the talking bridge. Well into the song, Presley stops singing and begins to speak as though he is the person that the song is about. He tells the story of his broken heart and the girl who left him behind before he launches into the final chorus. Songs with talking bridges were quite popular in the 1920's, when "Lonesome" was introduced. Talking bridges were also a trademark of the Ink Spots, one of Presley's favorite vocal groups. And, in general, talking bridges were not uncommon in country-western music. But, talking bridges were not associated with rock 'n' roll or r & b. Interestingly, "Lonesome" also reignited an unusual music fad called "answer records" or "answer songs," a concept which was widespread in blues and r & b recorded music in the 1930's through 1950's. Several girl singers recorded "answers" to "Are You Lonesome Tonight?" in which the girl who broke the heart of the singer offers her side of the story—in song form, of course. At least eight singers recorded their answers to Presley's musical question.

"It's Now or Never" was based on a well-known Italian song titled "O Sole Mio" ("Oh My Sun"). In 1949, American singer Tony Martin recorded a pop music version of "O Sole Mio" called "There's No Tomorrow." Presley liked the Martin rendition, but he wanted new lyrics and a new arrangement of the tune before he was willing to record it. Presley's version was titled "It's Now or Never," and it became one of his signature songs. Later that year, Presley recorded another song that was based on an Italian tune. "Surrender" is a modern version of "Come Back to Sorrento" ("Torna a Surriento"), which had been recorded by American pop singer Dean Martin, whom Presley had always admired. Because "Surrender" is less than two minutes long, it has the distinction of being one of the shortest songs ever to reach number one on the pop charts.

The music Presley recorded in the spring of 1960 represented a turning point for his career. Though some of the songs, such as "Stuck on You," are in the style of his 1950's music, some are clearly a departure, such as "It's Now or Never" and "Are You Lonesome Tonight?" The new music was smoother and less controversial than the pre-army material.

Presley changed his style of music for several reasons. One reason was simply personal taste. Presley liked many styles and genres of music, including pop. He did not think it unusual to include pop and rock 'n' roll on the same album, just like he did not think it odd to break into a gospel classic at a concert where his fans were expecting rock 'n' roll. Another reason his style and song selection became more pop-oriented was because a smoother style of music made a comeback among new young singers during the early 1960's. The hard-driving rhythms of Chuck Berry, Jerry Lee Lewis, and Little

Richard—who had become popular in the wake of early Presley—were no longer as prominent as they had been. Instead, clean-cut, well-dressed American male singers, such as Bobby Darin, Fabian, and Frankie Avalon, crooned snappy love songs or slow ballads in an easy-going, melodic style. Finally, the new direction of Presley's music was also intended to help audiences forget the controversy of his earlier music and hip-swiveling performing style. Parker felt that Presley's identity as a rock 'n' roll rebel would limit his overall popularity. He wanted Presley to be attractive to adult audiences as well as teen-agers. So, he steered his client away from rock 'n' roll and toward the pop music that mature audiences listened to.

Over the next few months, Parker guided Presley's career in a new direction that attracted new audiences and gave him a fresh, more mature image than the one that caused him trouble during the 1950's.

ADULT LISTENING

On May 12, 1960, Presley appeared on television for the first time since his discharge from the Army. He was a guest on *The Frank Sinatra Timex Special*. Parker made the deal with the show's producers months before Presley was released from active duty. He hoped that appearing with famous American singer Frank Sinatra would introduce Presley as a pop singer to a wide audience made up of adults and pop music enthusiasts, teen-agers, and country-western fans. Never one to take chances, Parker packed the studio audience with 400 members of one of Presley's biggest fan clubs to make sure that Presley would make a big splash. Parker's plan succeeded because the program received record-breaking ratings.

Sammy Davis, Jr., Peter Lawford, and Joey Bishop also appeared

Presley and Frank Sinatra, left, performed each other's songs on The Frank Sinatra Timex Special *on May 12, 1960.*

on the television special. In addition to these members of Sinatra's famed "Rat Pack," the cast included Sinatra's daughter Nancy. The show was subtitled "Welcome Home, Elvis," and in the opening segment, Presley wore his Army uniform. Later, he changed into a stylish but conservative black tuxedo and joined Sinatra for a short duet. Presley sang Sinatra's "Witchcraft," while Sinatra crooned Presley's "Love Me Tender." In another segment, Presley sang both sides of his new single, "Stuck on You" and "Fame and Fortune." His choice of clothing and his new, shorter hairstyle in addition to his connections with established show business legends showed that Presley's career was taking a new direction. Sinatra had his own legion of shrieking teen-age girls in the 1940's when he began his singing career. After Presley and Sinatra sang each other's songs, it was as though Sinatra was passing on his status as the pop idol of one generation to the idol of the new generation.

On March 25, 1961, Presley performed live at the Bloch Arena in Pearl Harbor, Hawaii, as a benefit for the U.S.S. *Arizona* memorial fund. The U.S.S. *Arizona* was a battleship that had been sunk on Dec. 7, 1941, during World War II (1939–1945). The fund was set up to raise money to build a memorial to the sailors of the *Arizona* who had been killed in the attack. Ticket prices for this performance ranged from $3 to $10 (about $20 to $65 today), with 300 ringside seats reserved for people who donated $100 (about $650 today). Presley and Parker bought 30 special seats and donated them to patients from Tripler Hospital in Hawaii. Presley's benefit raised more than $62,000 (about $404,000 today) for the memorial fund. On March 30, the House of Representatives of the Hawaiian legislature passed special resolution #105 to thank Presley and Parker.

There is no doubt that doing the benefit for the *Arizona* memorial made Presley seem more acceptable to the adult audience that shunned him when he was a rock 'n' roll rebel. But his career was not the only reason Presley wanted to help. He had a sensitive, generous nature, and throughout his entire life, Presley gave freely to charities and other worthy causes, whether he received publicity for it or not. Four years after this benefit concert, while he was in

Hawaii filming *Paradise, Hawaiian Style* (1966), Presley visited the completed *Arizona* memorial and placed a wreath there.

After the 1961 concert in Hawaii, Presley did not give another live performance until 1969, and he made no television appearances from 1960 until December 1968. Throughout most of the 1960's, anyone who wanted to see Presley had to go to the movies.

LEADING MAN

Not long after Presley taped *The Frank Sinatra Timex Show*, he returned to Hollywood to shoot *G.I. Blues* (1960). The movie's story line is about a singer who is serving in the U.S. Army in post-World War II Germany. Producer Hal Wallis had his scriptwriters take details from Presley's own life to flesh out the script just as he had done with *Loving You* (1957) and *King Creole* (1958). In *G.I. Blues*, Presley's character is not only stationed where Presley was, but he is a member of a tank division just as Presley had been.

King Creole was the third and final film Presley made under his original contract with Hal Wallis. As soon as he and Presley got to Hollywood, Parker negotiated another three-picture deal with Wallis. In his new contract with Wallis, and in subsequent contracts, Presley received a handsome salary and a percentage of the profits. At one point during the 1960's, he was the highest-paid actor in Hollywood. Parker also did well for himself through his practice of complicating standard contracts with side deals and promotions. He also received a screen credit for most of Presley's feature movies, often as a technical adviser.

Though there are some similarities with his pre-army movies, *G.I. Blues* also includes some differences. For example, *G.I. Blues* is a musical comedy instead of a musical drama. The movie is aimed at a family audience, and Presley's controversial performing style has been toned down. He still moves freely when he sings, but a troupe of long-legged dancers do most of the hip-swiveling. Presley also plays a different sort of character—one who's older and whose manner seems more conservative. Although most of the songs in *G.I. Blues* are fast-paced, they lack the hard-driving sound and emotional delivery of Presley's 1950's rockabilly. His movie image has been deliberately softened. In one scene, he baby-sits an adorable infant. In another, he sings the German folk song "Wooden Heart" ("Muss I Denn") to children at a puppet show. Presley even sings part of the song in German; the song became a hit over much of Europe by February.

Presley's hair is relatively short in *G.I. Blues* compared to the wild "ducktail" of his earlier career. His hair is also a different color. After the Technicolor *Loving You* was released, Presley started to dye his hair jet black. Presley's natural hair color was dark blond or light brown, but it usually looked darker because of the pomade he used to slick it down. The blue-black hair was striking with Presley's eyes and complexion, and Presley felt that dark-haired actors, such as Tony Curtis, whom he admired, looked the best and had better staying power as movie stars. The two films that Presley made after *Loving You* are black and white, so the change in his hair color wasn't obvious. *G.I. Blues* and most of his other films during the 1960's were shot in color, and the deep tones of Presley's blue-black hair were more noticeable.

Despite Presley's new, wholesome image, *G.I. Blues* was banned in Mexico after his fans caused a riot at a theater in Mexico City. Moviegoers ripped out seats in the theater and also broke several windows. In addition to *G.I. Blues*, the Mexican government banned all future Presley films. But in the United States, *G.I. Blues* was enormously successful; it ranked 14th in box-office receipts for 1960. The soundtrack album, which included the rousing title song and "Wooden Heart," remained on the charts longer than any other Presley album. Film reviewers applauded the new Presley. They were glad his sideburns were gone and thought he would find plenty of new fans among adult audiences.

Presley did not share the critic's enthusiasm for *G.I. Blues*. He felt that there were too many musical numbers, and he believed that some of them made no sense within the plot. He was also concerned that the quality of many of these songs was not as good as the music from his earlier films. In addition, he was eager to attempt more demanding and serious roles.

Flaming Star, which was released in December 1960 by Twentieth Century-Fox, gave Presley the chance to prove himself as a serious actor. In this tense western, Presley co-stars with respected actor John McIntire and legendary Mexican movie star Dolores Del Rio. Don Siegel, who later won critical acclaim for his work on the original *Dirty Harry* (1971), directed the film from a script based on a popular novel by Clair Huffaker. Nunnally Johnson, a long-time Hollywood producer and screenwriter, co-wrote the script with Huffaker. Established composer Cyril Mockridge produced the background music.

In *Flaming Star*, set in 1870's Texas, Presley plays Pacer Burton, the son of a white settler and a Kiowa Indian. A Kiowa uprising forces Pacer to choose sides between the white settlers and his mother's people. The movie shows the prejudice Pacer experiences because of his half-caste status. It makes a strong statement about racism, which was an important issue in the early 1960's during the Civil Rights era.

Despite the important message and the participation of such film greats as Del Rio, Johnson, and Mockridge, *Flaming Star* was not a financial success. Audiences were disappointed because they expected Presley to perform several songs, when he actually sang only two. A four-song print had been shown to a preview audience, but it was never released, possibly because Siegel thought that so many songs would detract from the movie's serious tone. Siegel may have been correct from an artistic and political point of view, since the movie received many good reviews, but it was a box-office disappointment compared with *G.I. Blues*.

Presley got another chance at serious acting in the movie *Wild in the Country* (1961), one of his most interesting films. This modern-day drama set in the South was directed by Philip Dunne from a script by famous American playwright Clifford Odets. Presley stars as a young hothead named Glenn Tyler, who tries to straighten out his life after serving time in a juvenile hall. He grows close to three women who become important to him. Tuesday Weld plays an uneducated country girl who urges Tyler to stay with his own kind. Hope Lange co-stars as a psychiatric consultant who encourages Tyler to go to college to pursue a writing career. Millie Perkins plays Tyler's childhood sweetheart who puts his interests ahead of her own, encouraging him to get an education even if it means giving her up. The three women represent Glenn's past, present, and future.

No songs were included in the original script for *Wild in the Country*, but after the poor showing of *Flaming Star*, six musical numbers were shot for the film. Only four made the final cut. In addition to the title tune sung over the opening credits, Presley sings one song each to the three women in the film. Even with the musical numbers, the movie was a disappointment for Presley's fans. Like *Flaming Star*, *Wild in the Country* did not lose money at the box office, but it did not make much money either. Both Presley and Tuesday Weld earned the Damp Raincoat Award for Most Disappointing Performers of 1961 by *Teen* magazine. While this award would hardly ruin anyone's career, it showed Presley and Parker exactly what kind of movie Presley's most-devoted fans wanted to see and, after this, Presley did not take on any more dramatic roles until the very end of his acting career.

Presley returned to musical comedies with *Blue Hawaii* (1961), his most commercially successful feature. Chad Gates, the son of a wealthy pineapple-plantation owner, is nothing like the characters Presley had played in the past, except that he has just gotten out of the army. The plot involves Chad's reluctance to trade in his Hawaiian shirt for a business suit. Pressured by his parents to join his father in running the plantation, Chad chooses to play music on the beach with his Hawaiian friends. Scenes were shot at Waikiki Beach, Hanauma Bay, and Ala Moana Park. The movie also features a huge cast of colorful characters. In response to his fans' cry for more songs, *Blue Hawaii* was stuffed with 14 musical numbers, including the title song and one of Presley's biggest hits "Can't Help Falling in Love." Most of the songs fit well with the plot, and there is a wide range of styles from the very hip "Rock-a-Hula Baby" to the comical "Ito Eats."

The director, Norman Taurog, was a competent Hollywood craftsman whose best-known effort was *Boys Town* (1940). He worked on nine of Presley's films—more than any other director. Taurog was Presley's favorite director, partly because he was sensitive to the concerns of his star. *Blue Hawaii* was released during the Thanksgiving-Christmas holidays in 1961. It quickly grossed almost $5 million (about $32.5 million today). The soundtrack album was the fastest selling album of that year. Unfortunately for Presley, the success of *Blue Hawaii* restricted him to acting in musical comedies. Parker, Hal Wallis, and other members of his management team used the tremendous box-office figures to convince a disappointed Presley that this was the only kind of movie in which his fans wanted to see him.

After *Blue Hawaii*, Presley made 23 more movies, most of which were financial and popular successes. Even though Presley failed to become a serious actor, he did become an extremely popular movie star. And, while none of his films was ever an award contender, several were highly entertaining and well crafted.

There is no denying that Presley's films were formulaic. Not only were most of them musical comedies but Presley's characters were remarkably similar. His characters were never trapped in the everyday world of business or other professions. They never went to an office; they never sat behind a desk. Instead, his characters held jobs that allowed him to work outdoors, or were dangerous and adventurous. A typical profession was that of a race-car driver. Presley played a race-car driver in three films: *Viva Las Vegas* (1964), *Speedway* (1968), and *Spinout* (1966). Other daring, extraordinary occupations for his characters included a pilot in *It Happened at the World's Fair* (1963) and *Paradise, Hawaiian Style* (1966); a boat skipper in *Clambake* (1967) and *Girls! Girls! Girls!* (1962); a rodeo performer in *Stay Away, Joe* (1968) and *Tickle Me* (1965); a carnival worker in *Roustabout* (1964); a trapeze-artist-turned-lifeguard in *Fun in Acapulco* (1963); a photographer in *Live a Little, Love a Little* (1968); and a Navy frogman (a person trained and equipped with aqualungs for underwater operations) in *Easy Come, Easy Go* (1967). No matter what job his character held, however, each could also sing. Presley's characters, no matter what they did for a living, averaged nine musical numbers per film.

Ann-Margret starred with Presley in Viva Las Vegas *in 1964. The film featured several lively dance numbers. Many of the tunes were in the hard-driving style of Presley's earlier material.*

Another similarity among the films was the use of exotic locations or vacation spots as the settings. Only rarely were his films set in New York, Los Angeles, or small-town America. Sometimes his characters were only visiting or passing through these vacation towns, as in *Viva Las Vegas*, when his character arrives to enter his car in a race. Other vacation spots showcased include Hawaii, which was the setting for *Blue Hawaii; Girls! Girls! Girls!*; and *Paradise, Hawaiian Style. Follow That Dream* (1962); *Easy Come, Easy Go*; and *Clambake* were set in Florida. *Fun in Acapulco* was set in Mexico, while *Tickle Me* found Presley taking refuge at a dude ranch. *Double Trouble* (1967) landed the singer in London and Antwerp. Strikingly unusual settings include the carnival backdrop of *Roustabout*; the Indian reservation in *Stay Away, Joe*; the backwoods of the South in *Kissin' Cousins* (1964); a turn-of-the-century riverboat in *Frankie and Johnny* (1966); the racing milieu of *Speedway* and *Spinout*; and a 1920's traveling show in *The Trouble with Girls* (1969).

An interesting aspect of Presley's movies is the way they reflect the trends and fads of America during the 1960's. For example, when college students began to flock to Fort Lauderdale, Florida, during spring break of each year, Presley starred in *Girl Happy* (1965), in which he plays an entertainer hired to work in a club in Fort Lauderdale during spring break. When the world's fair came to Seattle in 1963, Presley starred in *It Happened at the World's Fair* that year. Hawaii became America's 50th state in 1959, and Presley drew attention to its unique beauty in *Blue Hawaii*.

Not all of Presley's movies followed a pattern, however. In *Follow That Dream*, for example, Presley played Toby Kwimper, a different type of character. The Kwimpers are a backwoods family who decide to settle on a stretch of beach in sunny Florida. They build a homestead right on the beach out of materials they find or salvage. Local officials try to force out the honest, down-home Kwimpers, who simply do not understand the complexities of the modern world. The comedy is a satire about the frustrations of our fast-paced, modern society, in which the simple pleasures of life have become obscured.

Presley was among several popular singers making musical comedies at this time. Pop stars and rock groups were appearing in musicals that appealed to young American audiences. Called teen musicals, these films featured everyone from Frankie Avalon and Annette Funicello, who starred in a series of beach movies, to the British rock group the Beatles, who appeared in the high-energy comedies *A Hard Day's Night* (1964) and *Help!* (1965). Presley's movies were a sign of the times.

By the mid-1960's, the Elvis Presley musical began to decline in quality due to poor scripts, tighter schedules, and lower budgets. Hal Wallis did not renew Presley's contract, and Parker sought other producers to finance his client's movies. As Presley's movies began making less money at the box office, Parker wanted someone who could work with lower budgets. Parker signed a deal with producer Sam Katzman to make two films, *Harum Scarum* and *Kissin' Cousins*. Katzman had earned the nickname "King of the Quickies" because he made films quickly for very little money by cutting corners. Each of the films that Presley made for Katzman was shot within three weeks, and the production values for each film were weak. Though Parker moved on to make deals with other producers and studios, the Katzman films represent a turning point. Afterward, Presley's films seemed weak and repetitive, and he grew increasingly discouraged about his acting career.

Whether good or bad, comedy or drama, repetitive or innovative, Presley's movies did what they were intended to do. They changed his image from a hip-swiveling rock 'n' roller to a mature leading man.

THE MOVIE MUSIC

Almost every film that Presley starred in during the 1960's was a musical. A soundtrack album was released for every movie and, after 1964, Parker suggested that Presley record only soundtracks. Aside from a gospel album and some fresh music recorded in 1967, the singer followed this advice. Many of the songs written for Presley's films were created by independent music publishers Hill and Range. These writers churned out tune after tune. They were merely picking up a paycheck. Typically, the music for the soundtracks was recorded as quickly as possible—often in two or three all-night sessions. In general, there are two things to be said about the movie music. There is a lot of it, because Presley averaged three films per year, and much of it is mediocre.

Presley recorded some forgettable songs during this time. Among them are "Queenie Wahine's Papaya" from *Paradise, Hawaiian Style*, "There's No Room to Rhumba in a Sports Car" from *Fun in Acapulco*, "Yoga Is as Yoga Does" from *Easy Come, Easy Go*, "He's Your Uncle, Not Your Dad" from *Speedway*, "Do the Clam" from *Girl Happy*, and "We're Coming in Loaded" from *Girls! Girls! Girls!*

No one was interested in making the music better, because the albums sold well enough on their own. Also, the albums promoted the movies, and movies served to remind people to buy the album. From a business standpoint, there was no reason to change the system.

Presley's movie music was a sort of rocking pop style. It was often fast-paced and rhythmic, like rock 'n' roll, but smooth, effortless, and easy to listen to, like pop. It was not revolutionary like his 1950's rockabilly sound, nor was it intense like his 1970's music would be, and it would be easy to dismiss the soundtrack albums.

However, there are a surprising number of good Presley tunes from the 1960's that should not be overlooked. For example, many of the tunes from *Viva Las Vegas,* including "C'mon Everybody" and Ray Charles's "What'd I Say," are in the hard-driving style of his earlier songs, and the title song, with its Latin-rock beat, is also infectious. Other excellent songs from this period are "Return to Sender" from *Girls! Girls! Girls!*, "Little Egypt" from *Roustabout*, "Rubberneckin'" from *Change of Habit* (1969), "Wolf Call" from *Girl Happy*, and "Can't Help Falling in Love" from *Blue Hawaii*. The latter became his standard closing tune for his concerts during the 1970's.

In recent years, Presley's 1960's music has been given a second life as part of the soundtracks for contemporary movies. For example, "Devil in Disguise" became the closing song for a 1989 comedy called *She-Devil*. And the entire soundtrack for *Honeymoon in Vegas* (1992) consisted of Presley tunes recorded by current entertainers. "A Little Less Conversation" from *Live a Little, Love a Little* was featured on the soundtrack of the 2001 remake of the Rat Pack 1960 classic *Ocean's Eleven* and remixed in 2002 by a Dutch deejay act called Junkie XL. After the song played behind a Nike World Cup commercial, it was released as a dance-mix single. The song was number one in more than 20 countries. Thus, almost 25 years after his death, a Presley song was in the Top Ten again.

ELVIS RETURNS TO HIS MUSICAL ROOTS

Presley's music almost disappeared from the charts during the 1960's. Between 1960 and 1968, he did not score one song on the country Top-Twenty charts. After 1963, his music never appeared on the r & b Top-Twenty charts again. In 1965, he had only one Top-Ten single, "Crying in the Chapel," which he had actually recorded in 1960. The following year, only one of his songs, "Love Letters," made it into the Top Twenty. Surprisingly, many of his soundtrack albums—even the forgettable ones—made the Top Ten album charts, but just barely. By 1967, none of his singles charted anywhere near the Top Twenty.

In 1966, Presley returned to his roots with the gospel album *How Great Thou Art*. Jake Hess, the powerful lead singer of the gospel quartet the Statesmen, put together an all-star quartet called the Imperials to back up Presley on the album. Hess and the Statesmen had been Presley's idols during the early 1950's, and Presley was delighted to work with Hess on the album. A high point on the album occurs when Presley and Hess duet on the Statesmen's famous "If the Lord Wasn't Walking by My Side." *How Great Thou Art* proved a milestone in Presley's career, winning him the first of his three Grammy Awards (presented annually in the United States to honor excellence in the recording arts and sciences) in the Best Sacred Performance category. Presley would win two more Grammys, also in this category. He won for the album *He Touched*

Me in 1972 and for the song "How Great Thou Art" from the album *Elvis Recorded Live on Stage in Memphis* in 1974. (It is ironic that Presley is most famous for being a rock 'n' roll singer, yet he never won a Grammy for that style of music.) Presley's relationship to gospel is best summed up by the singer himself: "Since I was two years old, all I knew was gospel music. That music became such a part of my life it was as natural as dancing. A way to escape from the problems. And my way of release."[1]

American record producer Felton Jarvis produced *How Great Thou Art* and he encouraged Presley to record more than only soundtrack albums. He recorded a handful of tunes in 1967 and 1968 that foreshadowed Presley's musical rebound of the 1970's. "Guitar Man," "U.S. Male," and "Big Boss Man" combined country music with a rock rhythm and beat, which sounded fresh compared with the music on his movie soundtracks.

Presley felt creatively energized by the new songs recorded with Jarvis. In 1968, he decided to stop making movies as soon as he fulfilled his last movie contracts. He wanted to go back to music.

The last three movies that Presley acted in were 1969's *Charro!*, *The Trouble with Girls*, and *Change of Habit*. Each of his last three movies differed from the musical comedies he had come to hate.

Charro! was a Western in which Presley played a tough, bearded gunfighter. Presley had appeared in only one other Western, *Flaming Star,* and that had been eight years earlier. *Charro!* was shot in 1968 and released in 1969. At that time, American actor Clint Eastwood's "spaghetti Westerns" (so called because they were Italian productions by director Sergio Leone) had become enormously popular. Spaghetti Westerns featured violent, tough cowboys who frequently double-crossed each other. Even the "good guys" were not heroic in the conventional sense. *Charro!* was written in the same style as Eastwood's spaghetti Westerns. Presley's character, Jess Wade, is a reformed "bad guy" who comes up against his old gang, who is terrorizing a small Mexican town. Wade uses a lot of gun power and violence to stop them. The unique part of the film is that Presley does not sing at all during the principle part of the story. He does sing the title song, but the music in the body of the film was not pop or rock 'n' roll music. It was written and arranged by American composer Hugo Montenegro, who had also created the music for some of the spaghetti Westerns as well as several American television shows.

The Trouble with Girls began shooting in the fall of 1968. There were a handful of musical numbers in the film, and it had comic bits, but the story also featured much drama. It was set in the 1920's in a *chautauqua*, a traveling tent show that provided education as well as entertainment. Presley starred as the manager of the chautauqua, who has to solve the many problems that plague his show. The story offered a slice of the American past, and there were a few subplots that did not involve Presley. Both of these elements were not typical of Presley's movies.

In his final big-screen appearance, Presley starred as a doctor who practices in an inner-city slum. A heart-warming drama with a strong cast, *Change of Habit* co-stars American actress Mary Tyler Moore as one of three nurses who are sent to help him. However, Presley's character is not aware that they are also nuns. Elvis sang only four songs in the film, which was very loosely based on the real life of a nun who had worked with children with speech handicaps. The director was a young man named William Graham who used various acting exercises to get his actors to create strong characters. According to Graham, Presley did very well in these exercises.

Many biographers and music critics have severely criticized the film career of Elvis Presley. Many believe his movie career weakened his musical output during the 1960's, and they tend to dislike most—if not all—of his movie music. There is also the assumption that because many of his films were similar in style and story that they all were bad. Presley himself made fun of his movies in his later life, and he often declared that he was disappointed in his film career. As he said, "I got tired of playing a guy who gets into a fight, then starts singing to the guy he's just beat up."[2]

However, Presley's opinion may have been based on the fact that he did not like musicals—the type of movie where the characters burst into song at any time and with which he was most associated. He had dreams of becoming a serious actor in dramatic roles, but those dreams were not realized. He grew more discouraged with each movie he made. Despite his personal disappointment, this does not mean his films were a waste of his talents. Also, simply because he wanted to be a serious actor does not mean he could have achieved this.

Biographers and others who criticize Presley's movies are generally those who preferred his rock 'n' roll image and music to his more conservative 1960's look and sound. They do not understand that these films were part of a specific time and place, nor do they understand why they were successful. Not only were these films financially successful, they made Presley a bona fide movie star. They also helped Presley become popular with mature, adult audiences, which was Parker's plan for his client from the beginning.

MARRIAGE AND FAMILY

Presley and his wife, Priscilla, had one daughter, Lisa Marie, born in 1968. The Presleys were divorced in 1973 but remained close friends.

On May 1, 1967, Presley married Priscilla Beaulieu. The marriage came as a surprise to both the public and the press. Priscilla had moved from Germany to Memphis to finish high school during the early 1960's, but Parker had shielded her from the press until she and Presley were ready to marry. The couple were married at the Aladdin Hotel in Las Vegas and then honeymooned in Palm Springs, California. The ceremony lasted just eight minutes and only a few of Presley's buddy-bodyguards were asked to witness the event. It was a surprisingly private affair for such a popular public figure. On Feb. 1, 1968, the couple's only child, Lisa Marie, was born in Memphis.

The years of Presley's marriage (1967 to 1973) were among the years of his last extended period of creativity.

Chapter 4: The World's Greatest Entertainer

In 1968, Parker announced plans for a Presley television special on NBC, which would air at Christmastime of that year. It was Presley's first television appearance in eight years. Parker planned for his client to sing several Christmas carols, a few ballads, and perhaps a novelty number. However, producer Steve Binder encouraged Presley to do something more daring. Binder hoped to capture what he believed had been Presley's greatest contribution to music, which was the adaptation of African American rhythm and blues to the mainstream tastes of young, white audiences. He wanted to show that Presley's original music had been essential to the development of rock 'n' roll. And, he wanted to prove that Elvis Presley was still the King of Rock 'n' Roll, his nickname since the 1950's. A battle of wills erupted between Parker and Binder, with Presley caught in the middle. Eventually, the singer—eager for a challenge—sided with Binder.

The special was called *Elvis*, though ads for the program often used the title *Singer Presents Elvis*, because Singer Sewing Machines sponsored the entire hour. After his death, fans began to call the program *The '68 Comeback Special*, because it revitalized Presley's career and pointed him in a new direction.

On the special, which aired on Dec. 3, 1968, Presley performed in four elaborate musical production numbers and two segments in which he sang live before a studio audience. Two of the production numbers illustrated the major influences on Presley's music. The one that focused on black gospel music and rhythm and blues opened with a modern dance interpretation of the spiritual "Sometimes I Feel Like a Motherless Child." Presley then appeared on stage to sing the gospel tunes "Where Do I Go But to the Lord" and "Up Above My Head," backed by the r & b trio the Blossoms. Presley, the Blossoms, and the Claude Thompson Dancers concluded the segment with a rocking rendition of Leiber and Stoller's "Saved," in which everyone declares that they used to "smoke and drink and dance the hootchy-koo," before they were saved from damnation.

Without a word of explanation, this musical production number suggested an evolution from gospel music to r & b to the music of Elvis Presley. It was a very clever use of music to make an important point about a singer who was one of the most significant cultural figures of the second half of the 1900's.

Another production number focused on the country-western influences on Presley's music, specifically honky-tonk music. This segment told a simple story through song and dance in which Presley—as the "Guitar Man"—roams the honky-tonk bars across the South looking for a chance to sing and play. Dressed in jeans, the Guitar Man begins his journey with little more than his guitar, which is indicated by the bluesy song "Nothingville." His adventures continue through song as he encounters carnival toughs in "Big Boss Man" and the temptations of women in "Little Egypt." The Guitar Man's increasing success was indicated through his costumes, which became fancier with each song. The costumes echoed the wild Beale Street clothes Presley wore in his 1950's concerts and films, suggesting that the story of the Guitar Man was his story. At the conclusion of the number, the Guitar Man walks off into a successful future—represented by a road paved with bright lights.

The special opened with Presley singing "Trouble" from his 1958 movie *King Creole*. The dramatic lighting and tight close-up of his face showed his lip curled up on one side of his mouth in what some people have called the "Presley sneer," a famous part of his image during the 1950's. Dressed in black, he looked every inch the dangerous rock 'n' roll singer of the previous decade. As he began a chorus of "Guitar Man"—basically, the theme song of the show—giant red neon letters spelled out his name in the background. The special closed with a song that pointed Presley to the future. This final number was similar to the large-scale sound that would define the next phase of Presley's career. "If I Can Dream" was a modern-day hymn with a gospel-style arrangement. The tune was written especially for him for the occasion. Dressed in a white, three-piece suit, which contrasted sharply with the black costumes he wore throughout most of the special, Presley sang the inspirational song against the red neon "ELVIS" sign from the opening number.

Presley starred in the television special Singer Presents Elvis, *which aired on NBC on Dec. 3, 1968. Presley performed in four elaborate musical production numbers and two segments in which he sang live before a studio audience. After his death, fans referred to the program as* The '68 Comeback Special, *because it revitalized Presley's career and pointed him in a new direction.*

For the live performance segments that were sandwiched between the production numbers, Presley wore a black leather suit, which has since become a symbol of Elvis Presley at the creative high point of his career. Designed by Bill Belew, who later created several of the famous white jumpsuits Presley would wear in concert, the leather suit with its high collar recalled the styles of the 1950's without duplicating them. His coal-black hair was fashionably long but combed back at the sides with the front cascading forward ever so slightly, reminding viewers of his hairstyle from 10 years earlier.

These two live segments offered a Presley who was older and more mature but still edgy and exciting. He referred back to the music of the 1950's but did not try to copy it. Most of all, the dynamic rock 'n' roller showed that he still had the star power to stir up the audience. Throughout the live segments, girls sighed, squealed, and swooned.

A MUSICAL REVITALIZATION

Shortly after *Singer Presents Elvis* aired, Presley returned to his hometown of Memphis in January 1969 to record the album *From Elvis in Memphis* at American Sound Studios. While there, he also recorded parts of a double album called *From Memphis to Vegas/From Vegas to Memphis*. American Sound was operated and co-owned by producer/engineer Chips Moman. Moman was in the midst of the most successful period of his career, during which he worked on 97 records that reached the music charts. Moman produced *From Elvis in Memphis* and sides three and four of *From Memphis to Vegas/From Vegas to Memphis*, as well as several Top Twenty singles for Presley, including "In the Ghetto," "Kentucky Rain," "Suspicious Minds," and "Don't Cry Daddy." Presley had recorded several songs with Felton Jarvis that were not related to movie soundtracks, but the recordings produced with Moman represented Presley's official break from the pop-music style associated with his film image. With a handful of notable exceptions (such as "Love Me Tender," "Jailhouse Rock," and "Can't Help Falling in Love"), Presley rarely sang in concert any of the 200-plus tunes that had been recorded in conjunction with his movies.

The musical style that emerged from the Memphis recordings was the basis of the sound he would become famous for in his Las Vegas and concert appearances. American Sound Studios influenced Presley's style through the musicians Moman hired to work at his studio. Presley felt a kinship with the musicians at American Sound that he did not feel at RCA's studio in Nashville. American Sound's house band consisted of young Southern musicians who had been inspired by Presley in the 1950's. Plus, Presley had personal connections with some of these band members, including guitarist Reggie Young and organist Bobby Emmons, who had played with Bill Black's Combo in the 1960's. He also knew drummer Gene Christman, who had worked in Jerry Lee Lewis's band. (Lewis was a fellow rockabilly performer from the 1950's, who had also gotten his start at Sun Records.) These musicians were younger than the musicians at RCA and, like Presley, they had also been influenced by blues and r & b. Their specialty was a sound called blue-eyed soul or swamp pop. It was distinctly Southern in flavor and became a significant influence on Presley's new sound and choice of songs.

The songs that were selected and cut for these albums at American Sound ranged from contemporary soul ("Only the Strong

Survive") to country tunes ("From a Jack to a King"). Some of the original compositions that Presley recorded had been written by a new generation of country music songwriters, such as Mac Davis and Eddie Rabbitt. Like the members of the house band, they had been influenced by Presley's 1950's musical style. Though diverse in genre, the songs were unified by their arrangements. The new music was a large-scale, fully integrated sound consisting of strings, horns, and background vocals by both male and female groups. This sound and style would be amplified to an epic scale during Presley's live concert performances over the next few years.

Like Presley's earlier music, this new sound was at once a combination of influences, yet somehow unique to him as a performer. The diversity of Presley's song selection also made categorizing his music difficult for journalists and reviewers who wrote about him. It was not country or rock 'n' roll, nor was it r & b. Yet, it was all of those genres at once. Eventually, they stopped trying to label it. It became simply "Elvis's music." Unlike his earlier music, it did not inspire others to follow in his footsteps.

The song "Suspicious Minds" represents the typical Presley tune from this phase of his career. Released in late 1969, it was his last number-one single. As produced by Moman, this fast-paced song with a hard-driving bass line blends a thundering sound of horns, strings, and drums along with the voices of Presley and a choir of female backup singers. The song begins to fade out, then slowly the volume builds back up, reaching a crescendo, then slowly fades out again, seemingly into infinity.

Presley ventured into the recording studio only occasionally over the next four years, and he recorded studio material only twice after 1973. His last Top Ten single was "Burning Love," released in 1972. RCA continued to release singles and albums of Presley's music, but much of it was recorded live during his concerts and Las Vegas appearances. The dominant image of Elvis Presley that emerged from the 1970's is one of the singer in concert. Though he did some important work in the recording studio, it was quickly overshadowed by the image of Presley in a white jumpsuit singing his heart out on stage.

In the early summer of 1969, Parker arranged for Presley to play the newly opened International Hotel (the name was changed to the Las Vegas Hilton in 1971) in Las Vegas beginning July 31 at a salary of $400,000 (about $2.1 million today) for four weeks, a remarkable amount at the time. Presley was nervous because he had not appeared before a live concert audience since 1961, a time when his music was much simpler. Also, the last time he had appeared in Las Vegas was 1956, when he had bombed.

For his return to live performing, he chose not to re-create his earlier image or sound but planned his act around the fuller sound of his new music. While his first band consisted of a guitarist, a bass player, and a drummer, Presley's onstage accompaniment in Las Vegas included the Imperials gospel quartet, a trio of backup singers called the Sweet Inspirations, a five-piece rock band, and a 38-piece orchestra. The large-scale musical support was due in part to the large room Presley was playing at the International. It seated 2,000 customers. Up to that time, only the biggest names in Vegas, such as Frank Sinatra and Dean Martin, could draw that kind of crowd. Presley was worried that he would not be a success. But Parker had all the confidence of a man who knew how to cut the best deal. He *knew* his client could fill the room. Parker was thinking ahead. After his client sold out the house every night, he planned to make an even better deal the next time around. He was so confident that he devised a new nickname to market his client—"The World's Greatest Entertainer."

Presley opened at the International on July 31, 1969, and the room was packed with tourists, fans, and celebrities. A variety of singers, composers, movie stars, and even Broadway performers showed up to watch Presley's first public performance in eight years. The celebrity list included Cary Grant, Paul Anka, Carol Channing, Fats Domino, Pat Boone, Ann-Margret, Henry Mancini, and Sam Phillips. Presley had personally invited Phillips to show his respect to the man who had first believed in him.

To the hard-pounding strains of "Baby, I Don't Care," Presley walked on stage. There was no emcee to introduce him. He grabbed the microphone, struck a familiar pose from the past, and snapped his leg back and forth. The crowd jumped on their chairs to give him a standing ovation before he sang one note. The audience of 2,000 began to whistle, applaud, and pound on the tables. When the ovation subsided, he launched into "Blue Suede Shoes" with the fury of a man on a mission.

Backstage after the show, many celebrities and well-wishers congratulated Presley on his triumph. However, the most meaningful moment of the evening occurred when Parker pushed his way through the backstage crowd. Where was "his boy" he wanted to know, which was what he had always called Presley. There were tears in the old man's eyes. As Presley emerged from his dressing room, the two embraced, too overcome with emotion to say anything. Colonel Tom Parker was a hard man to do business with, because he was often considered to be greedy and ruthless. He made mistakes with Presley's career, especially at the end. The relationship between Presley and Parker was complicated and not easy to understand. But there was a deep connection between the two men.

The next day, Parker sat down with the management of the International to discuss a new deal. The hotel offered Presley a five-year contract to play two months a year—February and August—for a million dollars per year. Parker had been right.

Following his success in Las Vegas, Presley took his act on the road. Parker arranged for him to appear at the Houston Astrodome in conjunction with the Houston Livestock Show and Rodeo. Presley set attendance records at the 40,000-seat Astrodome over the course of the six shows. Local reporters raved about the show and, for the first time in years, fans waited to mob him after a performance. They surrounded his limousine as he tried to leave the facility, shoving flowers and gifts through the doors and windows.

Presley's professional accomplishments lifted his spirits as well as his career. Matching these professional high points was a personal achievement in which he took a great deal of pride. In January 1971, Elvis Presley was named one of the Ten Outstanding Young Men of America by the national Junior Chamber of Congress (Jaycees), a nationally based community group devoted to civic duty. Presley was selected because of his generosity in donating to a number of charities—usually with no press or fanfare. He was so proud of the honor that he supposedly carried the award with him on every tour.

CONCERT KING

With the success of Las Vegas and Houston, Presley began a different phase of his career. He became completely associated with performing in concert. He played Vegas in February and August but toured throughout the rest of the year. By 1971, Presley was on the road more than most other acts in show business. He would tour for three weeks at a time, taking no days off and doing two shows on Saturdays and Sundays. He rested for a few weeks, then repeated the cycle. Presley generally played one-night stands, meaning every performance was scheduled for a different arena. Often Presley and his entourage arrived in a city and departed in less than 24 hours.

To some of his fans, nothing symbolizes Elvis Presley like his white jumpsuits. This is such a common image of Presley that those who don't know much about him might think he dressed like that for most of his career. However, the white costumes with their multi-colored jewels were part of only the last seven years of his career. As the 1970's progressed, the costumes became more elaborate—even gaudy—by incorporating chains, studs, wide belts with mammoth buckles, and real gemstones into their designs. Weighing between 25 and 75 pounds (11 and 34 kilograms) with cape, the jumpsuits were sometimes accentuated by waist-length or floor-length capes with brightly colored linings. The extremely high collars and widely belled pant legs added to their theatrical appearance. Later costumes were manufactured in brighter colors—powder blue, red, or bright blue trimmed with black. A few deviated from the plunging, v-shaped neckline and high collars to feature a vest-and-slacks design. Specific symbols associated with karate (which Elvis had studied since 1959), or images of strength and power—such as the eagle, the tiger, the lion, and the firebird—were emblazoned in stones and gems on the backs of these jumpsuits. Later, fans informally assigned names to specific costumes as a means of differentiating between various

Presley concert tours or Las Vegas appearances. The most readily identifiable costumes include the American Eagle, the Mexican Sundial, the King of Spades, the Inca Gold Leaf, the Red Lion, the Peacock, the Gypsy, and the Indian suit.

Presley's repertoire of songs varied somewhat throughout the 1970's. He added new songs that he liked, but the format of his act did not change. His band and orchestra began each performance with the opening strains from German composer Richard Strauss's symphonic poem "Thus Spake Zarathustra," also recognizable as the "Theme from 2001: A Space Odyssey." (*2001: A Space Odyssey* was a popular 1968 science-fiction film by American director Stanley Kubrick.) A kettle drum solo signaled the conclusion of "Zarathustra," and then turned into the driving rhythms of "See See Rider" as Presley bounded onto the stage. He then strutted back and forth in front of the audience to show off his latest costume. Whipping off his cape and grabbing a guitar, which he rarely played but used more as a prop, Presley then began singing the chorus to "See See Rider."

For the finale, he generally sang the ballad "Can't Help Falling in Love," which slowly built up to the large-scale sound typical of his style from this period. At the beginning of this number, Presley resumed wearing his cape, signaling the end of the show for the band and the audience. He often concluded the number by dropping to one knee, grabbing the ends of the cape in his hands, and spreading the width of the garment to resemble wings. He raised his arms slowly upward while bowing his head—like an angel ascending into heaven or a great bird about to take flight. Presley then left the stage area and exited the building altogether, while the band closed the show with a reprise of "See See Rider." He never returned for an encore; it would be difficult to follow such an intense exit.

"Love Me Tender" was designated as the love song to the audience, but Presley actually sang very little of the ballad because he spent most of the time kissing fans while the music played. Fans learned to line up as close to the stage as possible when they heard the opening notes to "Love Me Tender," in the hopes of kissing or touching Presley. Those in the front row had the privileged seats, as they almost always received a kiss, or at least a handshake. However, sometimes the stage incorporated a runway, so that Presley could walk into the audience and interact with those not fortunate enough to sit in the front rows. In addition to kissing the women, he also threw dozens of scarves and towels into the audience. He used these during the show to wipe his brow. Though he threw an occasional towel or two into the audience throughout the evening, he gave them away one right after the other during "Love Me Tender." The audience got into the act—literally—by throwing a variety of gifts onto the stage for him. Often, bouquets of flowers were thrown or presented to him by the women in the front row. The exchange of gifts represented a sort of personal interaction that suggested intimacy between the performer and his fans. Presley was not afraid to touch, kiss, or hug any member of his audience, and he sincerely showed his appreciation for their affection. This closeness between Presley and his fans made them some of the most loyal fans in show business.

Other numbers in Presley's stage show also had a special significance, particularly "An American Trilogy." "Trilogy" combined "Dixie," "Battle Hymn of the Republic," and the spiritual "All My Trials" into a medley originally arranged and recorded by country singer Mickey Newbury in 1971. Presley recorded and released the medley as a single the following year, but the piece is most memorable as a showcase for Presley's large-scale musical sound and operatic performance style. The medley reflects several defining aspects of Southern history, with the Confederate anthem "Dixie" colliding with the Union's "Battle Hymn of the Republic," while the quiet strains of "All My Trials" echoes the civil rights movement of the 1950's and 1960's. The tempos of the songs in this arrangement are not traditional: "Dixie" has been slowed down, resulting in a lonely, wistful quality; "All My Trials" is rendered in a poignant whisper; and "Battle Hymn of the Republic" slowly builds to a powerful peak, which is the climax of the song. The piece conveys the trials and tribulations of the South as a battleground for the Civil War in the 1860's and for the civil rights movement in the 1950's and 1960's. Presley's dramatic performance of the medley—in which he bowed his head, dropped to one knee, and spread his cape to resemble a pair of wings—added a passion to the piece that other performers could never have achieved.

In June 1972, Presley played Madison Square Garden in New York City. This was the first time he had ever performed a concert in New York. All four shows were sold out, but Presley was concerned that the sophisticated New York music reviewers would not like his Vegas-style show. Presley was decked out in one of his bejeweled jumpsuits on opening night. The outfit included a gold-lined cape and a gigantic gold boxing championship-style belt emblazoned with "World's Championship Attendance Record." (The belt was presented to Presley by the president of the International Hotel during his engagement at the hotel in 1970.) Presley was in good physical condition. His performances during this period were often punctuated by dramatic karate moves and poses, and he continued to study karate to stay in shape. His voice was strong and clear, and he sang a variety of old and new songs with drama and flair. Presley need not have worried, because most of the reviewers were enthusiastic. RCA recorded two of the shows at the Garden for an album titled *Elvis as Recorded at Madison Square Garden*. The songs were mixed, the records were pressed, and the albums were in the stores in less than two weeks. The album went gold within weeks, eventually reaching triple-platinum sales of more than three million over the years.

MGM produced and released two documentaries that captured Elvis Presley's live performances. *Elvis: That's the Way It Is* is a feature-length movie filmed in 1970 during Presley's annual engagement at the International Hotel in Las Vegas. About half the movie features his performance on stage in the main room. The rest of the film documents the preparations for the show. Presley is shown in rehearsal for the show, whipping his band into shape and mastering new material. The film was directed by Denis Sanders, who had won an Oscar for a short film in 1954. *Elvis: That's the Way It Is* was released on Nov. 11, 1970, to good reviews. Two years later, MGM released another documentary about Presley, which had been shot in the spring of 1972. *Elvis on Tour* focused on his road show during a 15-city tour. The film captured the final phase of his career at its highest point. It was pro-

In January 1973, Presley returned to television with Elvis: Aloha from Hawaii. *The special was broadcast live via telecommunications satellite to several countries in Asia. It was the first time a commercial television special was broadcast over such a large area.*

duced by Pierre Adidge and Robert Abel, who had won acclaim for other rock documentaries. Some of the editing was supervised by a young Martin Scorsese, the award-winning American director who had also worked on the editing of *Woodstock* (1970), the most famous concert movie of the 1960's. *Elvis on Tour* won a Golden Globe for the Best Documentary of 1972.

In January 1973, Presley returned to television with a major spectacle, *Elvis: Aloha from Hawaii*. The show was a benefit for cancer research, and the proceeds from the concert went to the Kui Lee Cancer Fund of Hawaii. Presley's performance at the Honolulu International Center Arena was broadcast live via telecommunications satellite to Japan, Korea, the Philippines, New Zealand, Australia, Thailand, and other countries in Asia. It was the first time a commercial television special was broadcast over such a large area using the then-new satellite technology. The next day, a taped replay aired in Western Europe and, in April, the special was broadcast on American television. Over one billion people watched this performance. Dressed in his trademark jumpsuit with matching cape, Presley sang both new material and well-known hit songs. By the end of the show, he was so caught up in the enthusiasm of the audience that he hurled his cape, which was worth several thousand dollars, into the crowd.

The years 1969 through 1973 were an incredibly creative time for Presley. He returned to performing live and developed a new sound and a new image that completely replaced the singing movie star image that he disliked so much. Dressed in gold and jewels, this Elvis Presley lived up to Parker's title for him—"The World's Greatest Entertainer."

Chapter 5: The King Lives On

When Presley first gained recognition as a singer in the early 1950's, he enjoyed interacting with the fans who followed him. He genuinely appreciated their devotion and support. When they showed up at his house, he greeted them. If he was not at home, his parents, Vernon and Gladys, would greet them. Gladys even served them iced tea on occasion. As time passed, the attention of his fans overwhelmed him. He was mobbed, pushed down, and sometimes stripped bare by crowds of adoring fans. Presley could not sightsee, eat in a restaurant, or enjoy himself in public without his fans pouncing on him. By the early 1960's, he had begun living as a recluse. He secluded himself at Graceland or his home in California. Contributing to this sense of isolation was Presley's habit of sleeping all day and staying up all night. Because this schedule was out of step with most of society, Presley became somewhat out of touch with the real world. The isolation, combined with his boredom when he was between projects, eventually led Presley to develop some self-destructive habits.

THE DARK SIDE OF FAME

Presley's self-destructive habits worsened during the 1970's, after he returned to performing in concert and leading a hectic, rootless life on the road. His worst problem was his dependence on certain prescription drugs. Presley had several health problems, including back pain, weight gain, digestive troubles, and several eye afflictions. Treatment for these conditions put him in the hospital several times between 1971 and his death in 1977. He was also hospitalized for throat ailments, pleurisy (an inflammation of the lining of the lungs), and hypertension (high blood pressure). He abused the prescription drugs used to treat the ailments, particularly pain medication and diet pills. These drugs often left him in a state of mental confusion or led to erratic behavior.

Presley's lack of connection with the real world also contributed to his erratic behavior. His behavior was not extreme, but it was unusual by normal standards. For example, he was a generous man who frequently gave to many charities. However, his impulse to give often took a strange twist, and he would give outrageous gifts to complete strangers. Once, while he was buying several El Dorado automobiles for the members of his entourage, he noticed a couple wandering around the car lot looking for a car they could afford. Presley told them to select any car they wanted, and he would pay for it. He wrote out a check to the salesman and left him with the paperwork. On a trip to Colorado, he gave away seven Cadillac and Lincoln automobiles. When a local disc jockey heard about the caper, he joked on the air that he would not mind having a sports car himself. The next day, a Cadillac Seville was delivered to the deejay courtesy of Presley.

One of the most notorious episodes involving Presley's unusual behavior is not about his generosity, however. Instead, it had to do with the privilege that he believed he was entitled to because of his fame. The decades of stardom and adoration by the public had resulted in an exaggerated sense of self-importance. He was accustomed to having other people arrange their schedules around his, and he believed he could drop in on anybody at anytime. On Dec. 21, 1970, he dropped in on U.S. President Richard Nixon. Presley arrived in Washington, D.C., then drove by the White House and hand-delivered a letter requesting to see the president. Nixon cleared his schedule, and Presley—wearing a purple crushed-velvet suit and an Edwardian jacket draped like a cape around his shoulders—was allowed into the White House to see President Nixon that same morning. While visiting the president, he asked for a badge from the Bureau of Narcotics and Dangerous Drugs to add to his police badge collection. President Nixon gave it to him despite the objections of Deputy Narcotics Director John Finlator.

There were other downsides to being famous. Presley received many death and kidnapping threats during his career, but they increased during the 1970's. In 1970, an anonymous caller got through to his hotel room in Las Vegas and warned him that there would be an assassination attempt during that evening's show. Later that day, Presley received a menu from the International's dining room with his picture on the front. His likeness had been defaced, and a handgun was drawn next to his heart. A scribbled note by the drawing read, "Guess who, and where?" The FBI was called in, and the hotel management told him he did not have to go on. Though nervous, Presley went on stage anyway. On another occasion, in 1973, four inebriated, overzealous fans bolted onto the stage at the Las Vegas Hilton (formerly the International) during one of Presley's midnight shows. They began to get out of hand, but Presley's father, Vernon, four of Presley's buddy-bodyguards, and one of Parker's assistants dragged three of the men offstage. Presley knocked the fourth man off the stage himself and sent him hurtling into the crowd. Then Presley apologized to the audience, telling them he was sorry—that is, he was sorry he did not break the man's neck. The audience gave him a seven-minute standing ovation. There were other threats and incidents over the years, all of which point to the high cost of fame.

Presley's return to the road and the effects of his enormous fame probably contributed to the end of his marriage to Priscilla. Gone from Graceland much of the time while touring, Presley saw less and less of his wife and young daughter, Lisa Marie. The pace of performing in a different city every night made traveling together difficult, and touring was no life for a child. Priscilla left Presley in early 1972, and Presley sued for divorce the following August. In October 1973, the couple was officially divorced, but they remained close friends. They held hands during the divorce proceedings and walked out of the courtroom arm in arm.

By the time of the divorce, Presley's lifestyle, fame, and self-destructive habits had taken their toll. His health began to decline even though he was only in his late 30's. He led an increasingly secluded life inside the walls of Graceland, where there was no one with enough influence to discourage his self-destructive behavior. His weight became more of a problem, and he began to appear in concert overweight and out of shape. The press picked up on this and commented regularly on his bad appearance. He lost interest in recording new material, and his stage shows grew repetitious. His performances were sometimes weak. He stumbled over the lyrics to some of his songs, stopped and started certain songs over again, and lost his train of thought when talking to the audience.

While family members, friends, fans, and biographers have debated the quantity and type of drugs Presley took, the truth is that he simply took more drugs than his body could withstand. Elvis Aron Presley died at Graceland on Aug. 16, 1977. He was 42 years old. Found slumped over in the bathroom, Presley was rushed to Baptist Memorial Hospital where attempts to revive him failed. His personal doctor, Dr. George Nichopoulos, pronounced him dead. He announced the official cause of death as *cardiac arrhythmia* (erratic heartbeat).

THE KING IS DEAD

Presley's death had an immediate and major impact in the United States and across the world. The first reports were broadcast by Memphis radio station WMPS in mid-afternoon on August 16. As the news quickly spread across the country, many radio stations—from big-city rock 'n' roll outlets to tiny rural stations—began to play his music. Some quickly organized tributes to Presley while others played specific songs at the request of their listeners. Some people called their favorite radio stations simply to talk about the first time they ever heard a Presley record. Others recalled the sensation he created when he first shook his hips on national television years before. This outpouring of personal recollections from across America showed that Elvis Presley and his music had had a strong influence on American culture. So much so that, decades later, people could remember in detail how he had affected their lives.

Fans of rock 'n' roll, country music lovers, people who had been teen-agers in the 1950's, Southerners, and others were all in shock at the loss of a figure who had long been a part of their lives. The news of Presley's death became a "flashbulb moment"—an event that is so significant that people can recall exactly where they were and what they were doing at the time they heard the news. Just as many Americans could remember what they were doing and where they were when they heard about the assassination of U.S. President John F. Kennedy in 1963, so could many recall the day Elvis Presley died.

Within an hour of the news of Presley's death, fans began to gather in front of Graceland. By the next day, when the Music Gates were opened for mourners to pay their last respects, the crowd had grown to 20,000. By the time Graceland closed for the day, 80,000 people from across the country had viewed the body.

That initial gathering at the Music Gates was the start of a tradition that has continued in the more than 25 years since Presley's death. Each August, fans travel to Memphis from all over the world to commemorate the death of Elvis Presley but also to celebrate his life and accomplishments. On the evening of August 15 each year, they line up outside the Music Gates and swap Presley stories. At 11:00 p.m., two or more Graceland employees walk down to the gates with a torch. They open the gates for the crowd, who carry candles as they file past the gravesite behind the main house. The ritual is known as the Candlelight Vigil, and its roots can be traced back to the outpouring of grief by those who had first gathered at the gates at the time of his death.

Presley's casket was taken from Graceland to Forest Hill Cemetery in Memphis in a white hearse, which was accompanied by a long caravan of all-white automobiles. Less than two months later, his body was reburied at Graceland.

The funeral was held on August 18, and the event was fit for the King of Rock 'n' Roll. Fans had sent a tremendous number of flowers to Graceland, and the staff set them up in front of the house. Thousands of arrangements were delivered, and many of them were shaped like guitars, stars, and hound dogs. Many of the arrangements were sent on to Forest Hill Cemetery, where Presley was to be buried. There they sat alongside more humble arrangements, such as hand-picked flowers in soda bottles. After the funeral, Vernon Presley allowed the fans to take away the flowers as mementos.

The funeral was a small affair attended by many celebrities, including Presley's long-time friend, actress Ann-Margret, country music artist Chet Atkins (who had been one of Presley's music producers), and Sam Phillips. Gospel performers Jake Hess, J. D. Sumner, and James Blackwood and their vocal groups sang, as well as Kathy Westmoreland, who had been one of Presley's backup singers in his concerts.

The casket was taken from Graceland to Forest Hill Cemetery in a white hearse, which was accompanied by a long caravan of all-white automobiles. The caravan had a police escort, and several officers stood by to help with crowd control. There are photos and news footage of policemen saluting the hearse as it slowly drove by them. Presley had always been a supporter of policemen and their work. He liked to collect police badges from different cities and from various law enforcement agencies. He was close friends with many of the Memphis police, and he often contributed money to the families of officers killed in the line of duty. The officers saluted as a sign of respect.

Presley's body was originally buried at Forest Hill. However, because of the possibility of damage to the cemetery by throngs of fans and the threat of body-snatching by vandals, his remains were removed. His and his mother's brother's bodies were reburied in the area on the grounds of Graceland known as Meditation Garden. Later, the bodies of his father, Vernon, and his grandmother, Minnie Mae, were buried in the garden. The little family who had struggled together when Presley was young, and who had experienced his success when he became famous, were now together in death.

LONG LIVE THE KING

Not all of the events and publicity surrounding Presley and his death were positive outpourings of grief, respect, or admiration. On Aug. 1, 1977, just a couple of weeks before he died, an unauthorized biography of Presley was published. Written by three former bodyguards who had been fired the year before, the book discussed Presley's prescription drug abuse for the first time. It also offered a look at the dark side of his enormous fame and fortune. In an odd coincidence, a newspaper column about the

book was published on the same day that Presley died. The timing of the book, the column, and Presley's death brought the negative stories into the spotlight.

Immediately after Presley's death, record stores across the country quickly sold out of his recordings. RCA's pressing plants (where records and tapes were duplicated) operated 24 hours a day to keep up with the new orders for Presley's records. For a while, RCA hired pressing plants that they did not own in order to keep up with the demand. This was not only true in America but also in Europe. In Germany, where Presley had always been popular, one factory stopped pressing the records of all other artists until factory workers caught up with the Presley orders. By October, sales of Presley records were so high that some of his albums were on the music charts again.

While it may seem unusual that an entertainer who has died could continue releasing new records, that was just the case with Elvis Presley. Many of his concerts and Las Vegas performances had been recorded by RCA, so the company had a huge collection of live material to draw from. Also, RCA had always saved any additional recordings by Presley that were not included on the final version of his albums, and they released this material. Later, after RCA was sold to a larger company called BMG, some of the executives there

Presley is buried in Meditation Garden at Graceland, shown above, *along with his parents and grandmother. Note that Presley's tombstone bears the "corrected" spelling of his middle name. When Presley was an adult, he considered legally changing the spelling to the more biblical "Aaron." When Presley died, his father chose Aaron for the tombstone.*

understood the historical importance of Elvis Presley. They remastered his old recordings and released them in the best condition possible so that new generations could appreciate the music of Elvis Presley. They released CDs and compilations of his music in a historical context to help explain why his music was so important to our culture. In doing so, they helped younger generations to understand that the true legacy of Elvis Presley is his music.

In 1982, Priscilla Presley, who became executor of the Elvis Presley estate, and others who were on the board of directors, decided to open Graceland to the public. This gave the fans a place to congregate when they came to Memphis, and the festivities surrounding the anniversary of his death grew larger. Today, over a half million tourists from around the world visit Graceland each year. Elvis Presley Enterprises, now owned by Elvis's daughter Lisa Marie, is a multimillion dollar industry, operating everything from a hotel to a clothing line. In 2006, Graceland was designated a National Historic Landmark. This designation is given by the U.S. Secretary of the Interior to sites where significant historical events occurred, or where prominent Americans worked or lived, and represent the ideas that shaped the country.

The loyalty of Presley's fans and the continued marketing of his records make for a remarkable story, but most importantly, they reveal the impact that Elvis Presley has had on American society. His music, his performing style, and his connection to teen-age audiences challenged and then changed the culture of America. Later, his ability to alter his style and music to appeal to larger audiences demonstrated his immense talent as an entertainer. In death, the legendary stories, the bad publicity, the continued popularity of his music, and the loyalty of his fans have turned Elvis Presley into a myth that shows no signs of fading away. ■

Mick Jagger (1943–   )

For more than four decades, audiences have watched Mick Jagger front the Rolling Stones—"The Greatest Rock 'n' Roll Band in the World." As the band's lead singer and spokesperson, he has entertained, thrilled, and shocked the public over the years. Jagger has interpreted the songs of the Stones through his unique vocal style, and he has also helped compose some of their most memorable hits. In doing so, he has attracted fans to the band's blend of rock 'n' roll and blues.

In the early 1960's, the Rolling Stones combined the music of African American blues artists, such as Muddy Waters, with the rhythm of rock 'n' roll. The resulting style has outlasted many popular music trends and fads that frequently grab the spotlight but add little to the culture. Jagger's aggressive and sensual performing style was an extension of the unrestrained sexuality of such dynamic performers as Muddy Waters and Elvis Presley, but the English singer's brisk prancing is clearly a style all his own. Jagger has been equally expressive on stage and off. His unchecked lifestyle off-stage and uninhibited performing style onstage embody the spirit of rock 'n' roll rebellion first captured by Presley in the 1950's, while his hard, raw delivery echoes the intense blues style of Waters from around the same era and slightly earlier.

EARLY LIFE AND CAREER

Michael Philip Jagger was born to Eva and Joe Jagger on July 26, 1943, in Dartford, Kent, England. He grew up in the same neighborhood on the same block as Keith Richards, his future partner and bandmate. Mike, as he was then known to his friends, was between 5 and 7 years old when he first met Richards, but the Richards family would soon move to a housing project on the other side of town. The two lost touch until they were teen-agers.

Joe Jagger's given name was Basil but, as a young man, he began asking family and friends to call him Joe. He believed the name was more suitable for an athlete, which Joe had become. He had excelled at sports in school and, after attending Manchester University, and then King's College, London, he took a job as a physical education teacher in Dartford. When he applied for the job, he wrote that he wanted the chance to study "physical education in detail . . . providing insight, understanding and knowledge of man's movement, perform- ance and behaviour in sport and recreation."[1] His son Mick's later insistence on exercise to stay in shape for his grueling, physically drain- ing tours is evidence of his father's influence. Eva Scutts Jagger, from whom Mick would inherit his famous full lips, was the dominant fig- ure in her house as a young woman. She was organized and deter- mined. She kept the family's humble home tidy and filled with small, decorative touches, an indication of her determination to have a better life. Joe and Eva were married in 1940. In 1947, a second son—

Christopher—was born to the Jaggers. As the turbulent 1940's gave way to the more stable 1950's, the Jaggers found themselves living a comfortable, middle-class existence.

As a young boy, Jagger went to the local Wentworth Primary School. In 1954, he entered Dartford Grammar School after passing the difficult entrance exam. He was interested in history and in becoming a long-distance runner. Not long after, he formed a new interest— American popular music. He began to lis- ten to *rhythm and blues* (blues-based rock 'n' roll, also called r & b) and rock 'n' roll, developing an honest passion for the music. Later he recalled, "It seemed like the most real thing I'd ever known."[2]

Jagger played cricket as a schoolboy in England. He is shown (front row, right, seated) *with the Dartford Grammar School cricket team in 1955.*

KINDRED STONES

By 1961, Mick, as he was now known, had graduated from Dartford and gained entrance to the London School of Economics. One day, on the train into London to attend school, he recognized Keith Richards, and the two struck up a conversation. On the surface, Richards and Jagger seemed an unlikely pair to be friends. Richards's family had not been as financially secure as the Jaggers. His father was a foreman in a factory, and they had lived in a poorer section of town. When the two met again on the train to London, Richards was an art student while Jagger intended to study economics. Jagger was carrying a pile of records—including Muddy Waters and Chuck Berry albums—under his arm. The pair discovered they shared something in common—a passion for American r & b, blues, and rock 'n' roll. As the decades unfolded, their friendship and partnership grew into an exciting dynamic in which their differences complemented each other.

Jagger had been singing in a local Dartford band called Little Boy Blue and the Blue Boys. The name derived in part from the band members' interest in the blues. In London, Jagger began to frequent small clubs with Richards and bandmate Dick Taylor. One club in particular proved to be important to them. In 1962, English blues musicians Alexis Korner and Cyril Davies opened a basement establishment that they called the Ealing Jazz Club. As musicians, Korner and Davies took their sound from American bluesmen John Lee Hooker, Big Bill Broonzy, and Memphis Slim. They hoped to import these types of performers as acts in their club. There, Jagger and Richards met a musician who could play the blues guitar, complete with slide. He was calling himself Elmo Lewis, but his real name was Lewis Brian Hopkin-Jones (he went by Brian Jones).

Korner's tiny club nurtured the interests of the three budding musicians, providing a place where they could listen to blues and r & b, share their opinions on music, and finally come together as a band. Jagger began singing there with Korner's group, Blues Incorporated, which helped him to hone his skills and to overcome stage fright. A loose sub-group of Blues Incorporated formed at the club, with Jagger, Richards, Taylor, and a couple of other young musicians. Sometimes Brian Jones joined them, and sometimes Charlie Watts played the drums for them. Jones wanted to form a more official band, one that he would be in charge of. He gathered together a group of musicians he knew or auditioned, including Jagger and Keith Richards. He dubbed the band the Rollin' Stones after a Muddy Waters song they all admired, "Rollin' Stone." (The band's name was changed to the Rolling Stones when they were signed to Decca in 1963.) Jones was the force behind the band's formation, but quite quickly, the charismatic and confident Jagger became the Stones's front man. And, right from the beginning, this created tension between Jones and Jagger. The Stones's first official engagement occurred on July 12, 1962, at the Marquee Club in London. Their sound was very blues-influenced, with Jagger's vocals hard and raw. Sometimes he moved freely on stage, flipping his considerable head of hair, but at other times, he remained still while he sang.

Jagger was still trying to study economics by day while playing clubs at night. He was having difficulty deciding whether to give up the former for the latter. As he struggled with the decision, his grades suffered. His parents were against him abandoning his studies, and they pressured him to stay in school. In August 1962, Jagger left home permanently to live in London with Jones and Richards but he still tried to make a go of it at school. Each morning, he got up early, dressed in his suit, and attended his classes. When Jagger returned home in the afternoons, Richards and Jones, who had spent hours practicing their guitars together, were usually still sleeping. Jagger was smart and ambitious, and school meant something to him that it did not to Jones and Richards. He did not quit the London School of Economics until the summer of 1963.

The Rolling Stones recorded for the first time in 1962. The group pooled their money together to make an acetate on which they covered American r & b songs "You Can't Judge a Book by the Cover" (written by Chicago blues great Willie Dixon and made popular by Bo Diddley) as well as Muddy Waters's "Soon Forgotten" and Jimmy Reed's "Close Together." They sent a copy to a couple of record labels, EMI and Decca, but both rejected it. By 1963, the group's fortunes improved dramatically when they became the regular band at the Crawdaddy Club in Richmond, a suburb in southwestern London. The club's audience quadrupled after the Stones began playing there. The Beatles, who had made a name for themselves with their record "From Me to You," but were not yet superstars, came to hear the Rolling Stones on April 14. The two groups met after the Stones's performance and talked through the night. Four days later, the Stones attended a Beatles concert at the Royal Albert Hall in London, where they were impressed by the admiring screams of the female fans. Watching from the sidelines, Brian Jones murmured, "*That's* what I want."[3]

In May 1963, while the Stones were performing at the Crawdaddy Club, George Harrison told Decca executive Dick Rowe about his favorite new band playing there. Rowe, who had turned down the Beatles a year earlier, was desperate to remedy his mistake. He drove all day from Liverpool to Richmond to see the band and signed a deal with the Stones's manager, Andrew Loog Oldham, practically on the spot.

ROCK STAR

The first record released by the Rolling Stones was a single titled "Come On." It did not make the Top Ten and sold fewer than 100,000 copies. However, the Stones did manage to land an appearance on a British television program called "Thank Your Lucky Stars," but Oldham made them wear matching black pants and black-and-white houndstooth jackets. The appearance was not a success. Jagger realized something from this incident. The band was made up of very different individuals from very different backgrounds. Their common interest in the music was what made them a good musical band, but their individual personalities attracted a variety of fans to their music. From this point onward, they would not dress alike. They would not even dress up, which was an unusual decision in an era when most performers wore dress clothes in public, especially for television appearances.

The Rolling Stones wore their street clothes, which ranged from jeans to ruffled shirts, depending on the band member. In addition, they wore their hair very long—even longer than the Beatles.

The Rolling Stones appeared on "The Ed Sullivan Show" six times. They are shown above in their third performance on the show on Feb. 13, 1966. Brian Jones, right, was the force behind the band's formation, but Jagger, center, quickly became the Stones's front man. Jones died in 1969. Bassist Bill Wyman, left, was with the band from its beginning in 1962 until he retired in 1993.

Consequently, music magazines and newspapers began to call the Stones "scruffy," "dirty," and "unkempt." On the back of the group's first album cover, their manager stated, "The Rolling Stones aren't just a group; they're a way of life."[4] It was the start of their identity as being the bad boys of rock 'n' roll in contrast with the cleaner-cut Beatles. While the Beatles had a hit with "I Wanna Hold Your Hand," the Stones would later have a hit with "Let's Spend the Night Together." When the occasional brawl broke out at a Stones performance, it became big news and added to their notoriety. The press emphasized the rivalry between the Beatles and the Rolling Stones, perhaps even instigating it. Popularity polls conducted in June and September 1964 while the Stones were on tour placed the band ahead of the Beatles, a fact reported in the music magazines and newspapers. On the basis of this popularity, the Stones toured America for the first time that summer. They made a stop in Chicago to visit Chess Records, where they recorded "It's All Over Now." This would be the high point of their visit, which was marked by bad publicity and negative reactions to their appearances. During their visit to Chess, they met their idols, blues legends Muddy Waters and Willie Dixon, and rock 'n' roll great Chuck Berry.

The music of the Rolling Stones was not original at first. The band covered and tried to copy the music of black American blues artists and rock 'n' roll singers, but they contributed nothing original. When Jagger began to compose songs with Keith Richards, their music evolved into something different. It was still influenced by blues and r & b but, at the same time, it was distinctive. It grew into a full rock 'n' roll sound, though harder and more aggressive than the melodic tones of other English rock bands. By this time the band consisted of Jagger, Richards, Jones, Bill Wyman on guitar, and Charlie Watts on drums.

BRITISH INVASION MAVERICKS

There were so many English rock 'n' roll bands on the scene in the U.S. in the early 1960's that the phenomenon became known as the "British Invasion." Most of these bands dressed alike, looked well-groomed, and presented a clean-cut image to newspapers and music magazines. The Rolling Stones did just the opposite. They never dressed alike, always wore their hair an inch or two longer than the latest style, and talked openly to the press about the brawls and fights at their concerts. The Stones were the mavericks of the British Invasion. Jagger and Richards became the most prominent members of the Stones, with Jones starting to take a back seat in the band he had actually created.

The Stones's first appearance on "The Ed Sullivan Show" in 1964 did nothing to diminish the band's bad-boy reputation. Performing "Around and Around" and "Time Is On My Side," the band was deemed so lewd that Sullivan apologized to the audience for allowing the group on the air. He promised his viewers that they would never be back. However, due to popular demand, the Stones *were* invited back and performed on the show five more times.

While the Rolling Stones were comfortable playing the role of rock's bad boys, musically, they did not catch up to this image until 1965 when they released "(I Can't Get No) Satisfaction," a song written by Jagger and Richards. Richards had awakened in the middle of the night in a Clearwater, Florida, hotel room while the band was on tour in America, energized by an inspiration. He turned on a tape recorder and strummed a fast-paced, riveting blast on his guitar. Then, he returned to bed. The next morning, he played the guitar lick (musical passage) for Jagger and suggested a theme for the lyrics: "I can't get no satisfaction." Jagger spun the idea into a song about the band's life during the American tour, and the song was finished. Richards thought they could use "Satisfaction" as filler for an album, but he did not believe the song would make a major release. The band recorded the song at RCA Records' studio in Hollywood, California.

Richards never warmed up to the song, thinking it was too simplistic and too removed from the blues sound that he loved. However, the rest of the band thought it was among their best work. In the end, Richards's objections were overruled, and it was released as a single, first in America and soon after in England. "Satisfaction" shot up the charts to become the Stones's first number-one song in America.

The song was controversial, though not as troublesome as later Stones's releases. Many thought the lyrics were about love and sex, but they were deeper than that. The song represented Jagger's criticism of the empty, commercialized American culture that he was exposed to while on tour, as well as the repetition and boredom of life on the road. The explosive, angry rhythms of the music were an example of the hard rock 'n' roll the group had been moving toward, but it was faster paced, and the electric guitar sound was more prominent. The song also had an aggressive, "in-your-face" attitude. Finally, their music had caught up to their image.

On the heels of "Satisfaction" came "Get Off of My Cloud" from the album *December's Children (and Everybody's)*, and "Paint It, Black" from the album titled *Aftermath*. These songs were also massive hits for the band, becoming signature songs for them. Over 40 years later, they still retain their force and vitality. Their success continued with "Let's Spend the Night Together" and "Ruby Tuesday" from the *Between the Buttons* album.

At the heart of the band's sound was Jagger's vocal style and stage presence. His singing style was hard, harsh, and raw. The rest of the band occasionally backed Jagger vocally but only to bring out Jagger's voice, never to blend with it. It was a sound unlike the rich harmonies of other British bands, including the Beatles. The lyrics of their songs were considered daring for the time, because they were often more about sex than love. Or, they reflected unrest and unresolved turmoil rather than peace and understanding. Jagger's onstage antics embodied the essence of the Rolling Stones. He was fond of wearing very tight pants, or even tights, with long scarves and the occasional cape. He pranced, preened, and strutted constantly around the stage. Like Elvis Presley a decade before, Jagger moved to the music with force and power, but also with grace and style. He had a natural charisma and an unusual performance style that he had fine-tuned while the band was working out its musical sound. By 1965, the whole act—Jagger's stage style, the music, and the image—clicked.

Off stage, Jagger was often seen in the company of strikingly beautiful women. He began a relationship with British singer Marianne Faithfull, for whom he and Richards wrote a song called "As Tears Go By," which the Stones also later recorded. The couple was shown in the newspapers and magazines constantly, attending clubs, parties, or concerts. Thereafter, Jagger's relationships with high-profile women were regularly played out in the press.

THE BAD BOYS OF ROCK

By this time, the Rolling Stones were playing large concert performances—just like the Beatles. They were touring Europe and America regularly, though prominent British figures and politicians bemoaned them as representatives of contemporary English culture. Before they left for one of their American tours, a British politician told the newspapers, "Our relations with America are bound to deteriorate. . . The Americans will assume that British youth have reached a new low in degradation."[5] Jagger and Richards, and the other band members to a lesser extent, played to this image in press conferences. Once, they threw cream pies at reporters. Such antics brought the group millions of young fans, who were disillusioned and disappointed with their parents' generation: they had brought about war and corrupted politics, put up with an out-of-date class system, and maintained a system of stifling social rules and conventions that restricted freedom of expression. No wonder "Satisfaction" became the unofficial anthem of the burgeoning youth movement—not only in England but also in America.

In January 1967, that freedom of expression was compromised when the Stones were scheduled for another appearance on "The Ed Sullivan Show." Sullivan found the Stones's hit song "Let's Spend the Night Together" "objectionable" and demanded that the band change the chorus when they performed the song on the show. The Stones grudgingly acquiesced, appearing on national television with the altered lyrics, "Let's spend some time together," Jagger rolling his eyes each time he sang the substituted words. (It wouldn't be the last time the Stones were censored on national televsion. Nearly four decades later, two songs the Stones performed during the 2006 Super Bowl halftime show were censored by the ABC TV network and the National Football League [NFL]). The Stones's censored performance on the Sullivan show recalled the famous last appearance of Elvis Presley on the show a decade earlier, when his gyrations caused the network to show the performer only from the waist up.

The following month, Jagger and Richards were arrested for drug offenses. The offenses were relatively minor. Jagger was charged with possession of amphetamines, which were called "pep pills" at the time. In fact, Faithfull had a legal prescription for them. Additional charges were brought against Richards and another man who had been with Jagger and Faithfull at the time. The police found the drugs by raiding Richards's home, where Jagger and other friends and associates were staying. The drug raid may actually have been a set-up; the police may have been tipped off by a journalist eager for a hot story.

Thumbing their noses in the faces of authorities for four years resulted in unkind and unfair treatment. The performers received shabby treatment in jail and stiff sentences for relatively minor offenses. The press made up story after story, exaggerating and even concocting details about the raid. One outrageous story stated that the band members had been engaging in voodoo and black magic when the police arrived. Richards was sentenced to a year in prison for his offense, despite the flimsy evidence against him. Jagger received three months. On appeal, Richards's conviction was eventually overturned. Jagger's was upheld, but his sentence was changed to probation.

Though some say Jagger and Richards were unfairly treated, they had still flouted the law. To remind them that their involvement with drugs could have serious consequences, the appeal judge warned Jagger about future drug charges. "You are, whether you like it or not, the idol of a large number of the young in this country. Being in that position, you have very grave responsibilities. [In the future] if you do come to be punished, it is only natural that those responsibilities should carry higher penalties."[6]

Jagger and Richards played down the whole incident in public, but the experience seemed to throw them off. With Brian Jones, they spent about a week in Morocco to escape the harsh headlines. When they returned, the band produced a new album titled *Their Satanic Majesties Request* (1967). Jagger and Richards moved away from their core blues influence to embrace the psychedelic sound of the late 1960's. The album seemed heavily influenced by the Beatles's famous *Sgt. Pepper's Lonely Hearts Club Band*, because of its electronic sounds, whimsical songs, and oddly composed lyrics in free verse. *Satanic Majesties* also featured studio noise and dialogue in the background, which was a fad of the psychedelic era. The result was one of the band's weakest albums. Sales were small, and when their next album, *Beggars Banquet*, was released, *Satanic Majesties* quickly faded from the public's collective memory. *Beggars Banquet* featured "Stray Cat Blues," "Street Fighting Man," and "Sympathy for the Devil." The latter was composed by Jagger as an essay on world politics, though after the earlier rumors, it was sometimes misunderstood as a song about worshiping the Devil. In fact, it is a political statement about the sad state of the world—not a song about black magic.

ROLLING AWAY A STONE

Though Brian Jones had started the Rolling Stones, by the mid-1960's he had faded into the background. Jagger was considered the unofficial leader of the Rolling Stones. As the charismatic lead singer of the group, he received the most attention in the press. Jagger learned to play the press to create a personal image of a creative, mysterious artist. He gave lengthy interviews in which he talked much but revealed little about himself or the band. He knew the more mysterious he appeared, the more intrigued people would be by him. Also, as Jones stepped further into the background, Jagger stepped up to deal with the business end of the group. Jagger and Richards were the premiere songwriters, with Bill Wyman occasionally coming up with musical arrangements or riffs (melodic phrases or rhythms). By the late 1960's, Jones was contributing very little to the group.

Brian Jones had always been a troubled man who suffered from emotional problems. From the beginning, he and Jagger had never gotten along as well as Jagger and Richards had, which made Jones resentful and jealous. Drug use also contributed to his increasing personal problems, and he had been arrested twice on drug-related charges. During the recording of *Beggars Banquet*, Jones had rarely showed up to participate. In June 1969, Jagger, Richards, and Watts went to Jones's house and fired him from the band. The parting was friendly, considering the tension there had always been between Jones and Jagger. The band offered him a large settlement, and they all agreed that the official reason given to the press for his departure would be that Jones wanted to pursue his own music.

Within a month, Brian Jones was found drowned in his swimming pool. Jagger and the band were sincerely devastated by his death. Despite Jones's erratic behavior and troubled life, Jagger and Richards remembered that he had been a good friend and that he had been the driving force behind the band in its earliest days. Though Jagger missed the funeral because he was in Australia acting in the film *Ned Kelly*, he and the band hosted a free concert in Jones's honor. (The concert had already been scheduled, so rather than cancel it, the band used it as a memorial for Jones.) On July 5, 1969, the band gathered in London's Hyde Park to play music and recite poetry for their friend. Near the end of the event, they released 3,500 butterflies in memory of Brian Jones.

The band hired British guitarist Mick Taylor to help them out on their next American tour, which was scheduled for the fall of 1969. A new single, "Honky Tonk Woman," was released before the tour, and it became one of their most successful hits. Jagger was at the peak of his talents not only as a singer but as a performer. His stage presence was electrifying, particularly as he performed "Midnight Rambler" and "Jumpin' Jack Flash." But 1969 was not a good year for the Rolling Stones, and trouble followed them right up to the last month.

The Stones decided to show their appreciation for America by staging a free concert as the last stop on their tour. The concert was held at the Altamont Speedway just outside San Francisco on December 6. Badly organized, the concert turned into an extended affair in which thousands of fans waited around for hours for the acts to begin performing. The Stones were scheduled to go on last and, by the time they appeared, the crowd had become unruly. The Hells Angels, a California-based outlaw motorcycle club, had been hired to handle security—a mistake that ended in disaster. They assaulted fans, pushed them off the stage, and then stabbed a man to death. Many were critical of the Stones, and especially of Jagger. Some felt that Jagger's performing style excited people too much, and led to violence. Others noted that the band had always courted violence, and the speedway mayhem was a result of the content of their song lyrics and off-hand remarks to the press. Two American filmmakers, brothers Albert and David Maysles, were making a documentary about the Stones tour, and they caught the murder on film. Those who had not attended the concert could see the incident in the Maysles's documentary *Gimme Shelter* (1970), which extended the impact of the event. Altamont haunted the Rolling Stones for a long time—personally and professionally. They did not tour America again for over two years.

The Stones's free concert at the Altamont Speedway in California on Dec. 6, 1969, was badly organized and ended in disaster when a man was killed. The event was captured in the 1970 documentary, Gimme Shelter. Guitarist Mick Taylor, center, had just joined the band. Jagger is shown on the right, guitarist Keith Richards is on the left, bassist Bill Wyman is behind Taylor, and drummer Charlie Watts is seen in the mirror in the foreground.

THE GREATEST ROCK 'N' ROLL BAND IN THE WORLD

Despite the controversy, the Rolling Stones were approaching a creative high point. They started the new decade by announcing they were changing record companies, from Decca to Atlantic. As part of the deal, Atlantic agreed to create a label especially for the band—Rolling Stone Records (RSR). The logo for RSR became one of most recognizable images in all of popular music—a pair of full, bright-red Jaggerlike lips with a tongue sticking out. In 1971, the Stones released the first album on their new label, *Sticky Fingers*, which became a major hit. The following year, the critically acclaimed *Exile on Main Street*, which was heavily influenced by American blues, country, and gospel music, proved equally successful. In 1972, the Stones returned to America to tour. Fortunately, there was no backlash from the Altamont incident. Indeed, the tour was planned on a vast scale, and the Stones seemed to bowl over every town they visited. Stevie Wonder, a highly respected African American r & b musician, was their opening act. The band and their entourage traveled around the country in a private jet with the tongue logo of their record label painted on the side. It was the type of hype and theatricality on which Jagger thrived.

Jagger's personal life changed during this period. In 1970, he met Nicaraguan model Bianca Pérez. They married in 1971. A daughter, Jade, was born in October of that year. Around the same time, the band moved to France to avoid paying the heavy taxes they owed in their native country. For a time, the United Kingdom levied heavy taxes against high-income entertainers, and many actors, rock stars, and other performers found they could no longer afford to live there. Eventually the Stones—getting around U.K. taxes by becoming "citizens of the world"—moved back to the United Kingdom part-time, and continued to produce successful albums there at regular intervals. However, the Rolling Stones had grown older and more settled. Critics felt that the band had lost its innovative edge, and their music was becoming uninspired.

By this time, Jagger had pulled away from the band to a degree. As a charismatic lead singer, Jagger, like Elvis Presley in his early career, had attracted the attention of film directors. Jagger found a new challenge in another art form: film.

ACTOR

Mick Jagger acted for the first time in an unusual film called *Performance* (1970), which captured the bohemian flavor of the 1960's. It was directed by British filmmakers

Nicolas Roeg and Donald Cammell, who were attracted to Jagger's natural charisma. They felt that the singer's image as a self-absorbed rock star made him the perfect choice to play one of the film's main characters, a pop singer named Turner. Turner lived an extravagant and decadent lifestyle, and he was frequently depicted wearing makeup and dresses. It was not much of a stretch for Jagger, who himself was known to wear makeup on occasion. But, he surprised the directors with his serious, artistic nature and his professionalism. The film was shot in 1968, but it was not released until 1970.

To Jagger, acting was a lark, a creative break from singing and composing. Directors who cast him did so because of his image. As Mick Jagger, lead singer of the Rolling Stones, he was—and is—a celebrity associated with an extravagant lifestyle, beautiful women, and outrageous antics. In other words, no one would cast Mick Jagger as "the average guy who lives next door."

After *Performance*, he starred in the Australian film *Ned Kelly* (1970), the story of a legendary outlaw. Jagger was cast because he was—and still is—a maverick who lives outside the norms of society, just like Ned Kelly had. In a way, Jagger was a modern-day outlaw, especially during the 1960's and 1970's. Though directed by the well-respected British filmmaker Tony Richardson, the film did poorly when it was released in 1970. Jagger was disappointed in the results, and he did not attempt film acting again until the early 1980's. German director Werner Herzog, an internationally famous filmmaker, asked him to co-star in his epic production *Fitzcarraldo* (1982). The film was the story of the title character who becomes obsessed with bringing a ship across the Peruvian mountains so he can bring opera to the jungle. Jagger's part was that of the sidekick to Fitzcarraldo, who was to be played by American actor Jason Robards. The film was shot on location in Peru, and

Jagger has received critical acclaim for some of his acting roles, including his performance in The Man from Elysian Fields *(2001).*

Jagger, left, plays guitar on stage occasionally and on some of the band's recordings. Ron Wood, center, has been a guitarist with the Stones since 1974. Keith Richards, the Stones's guitarist since the band was formed in 1962, is shown at right.

the cast and crew encountered many problems. Herzog shot for weeks in the jungles, and the shooting schedule fell hopelessly behind. Robards became ill with dysentery, a disease of the intestines. Jagger also fell ill, though it was not as serious. When Robards dropped out because of his illness, Jagger also quit because he had prior commitments with the band and had grown weary of the project. Herzog reshot the film with Polish-born German actor Klaus Kinski playing the main character. Jagger's part was completely cut out of the film, as Herzog was so impressed with Jagger's performance that he could not envision any other actor in the role.

Footage from the edited sequences are included in a documentary about Herzog called *Burden of Dreams* (1982). The footage reveals that Jagger had a strong charisma and a natural instinct for acting. His stage performances with the Rolling Stones had helped him develop a compelling presence, which he knew how to turn on in public. This ability served him well on the big screen.

In 1992, he co-starred in *Freejack*, a science-fiction film about a race-car driver who dies but comes back to life in the future. Jagger plays a villainous bounty hunter who tracks down people for their healthy bodies for use with the brains of people from the future. Though a forgettable movie, Jagger claimed that he had a good time making an action film with firefights, high-tech weapons, and futuristic costumes.

Jagger liked to act in about one film every 10 years and, right on schedule, he co-starred in a drama called *The Man from Elysian Fields* in 2001. The film told the story of a writer who is in financial trouble, played by American actor Andy Garcia. The writer is hired by a male escort service run by Luther Fox, played by Jagger. Though Jagger's face is now lined and wrinkled, in *Elysian Fields* his creased face becomes him, perhaps because of the contrast to his sharply tailored suits and the graceful and elegant bearing of his perpetually thin body. Like Jagger, who seems forever young every time he sings "Satisfaction," Luther Fox is reluctant to give in to old age and uselessness.

In the 1990's, Jagger became involved in films in another capacity. He moved behind the scenes as a producer. He formed a production company called Jagged Films, which has been responsible for a handful of well-crafted films, including the critically acclaimed *Enigma* in 2001. Jagged Films has made few films, but it tends to finance and support small-scale dramas that have difficulty getting funding from the large studios.

ROLLING ON

In 1978, the Rolling Stones released *Some Girls*, which returned the band to the forefront of rock 'n' roll. The album drew on their blues roots but incorporated new music trends of the time, such as dance music and punk rock (rock music performed in an aggressive, rowdy style). *Some Girls* was also one of the Stones's most controversial albums. The title song, with its tongue-in-cheek socio-racial commentary, attracted the ire of the Reverend Jesse Jackson, while Stones purists felt their favorite rock band had "gone disco" with the dance hit "Miss You." In addition, the album's Andy Warhol-designed cover, with its unauthorized use of celebrity snapshots, caused legal snags. The album had to be pulled from stores and the cover replaced. Nonetheless, *Some Girls* became one of the band's biggest-selling albums, and it revitalized their career. By this time, British guitarist Ron Wood had joined the band.

Jagger also made some changes in his personal life. He divorced Bianca Jagger in 1980 and began a long-term relationship with Texas-born model Jerry Hall. The two married in 1990 and had four children together. Though their marriage was annulled in 1999, Jagger and Hall remain closely connected through their children.

The Rolling Stones became one of the first rock 'n' roll groups to let a large company sponsor their tour. Jovan, a perfume company, put up the money for the Stones's 1981 tour. The expense for mounting a large-scale tour had grown enormously since the early days, and sponsorship was a way to offset expenses. In exchange, the Jovan name appeared on stage with the Stones and also on their merchandise, such as the tee-shirts and programs sold at the concerts. Critics accused them of "selling out," especially because Jagger had always derided America's consumer culture. Today, corporate sponsorship of large tours has become standard procedure for most singers and bands.

In the mid-1980's, Jagger and Richards split up because of creative differences. Richards had battled drug addiction for many years, but he had beaten the habit by this time. Without the distraction of addiction, he became more dedicated to his music. And, he was unhappy with the increasing commercialism of the Stones sound. He wanted more creative control over the band, which led to the separation of the long-time friends and partners. After they parted ways, Jagger began a solo career. He released *She's the Boss* (1985), *Primitive Cool* (1987), *Wandering Spirit* (1993), and *Goddess in the Doorway* (2001). The albums were not well reviewed and did not sell well. They lacked the edge that Richards had always added to the Jagger-Richards pairing.

By early 1989, the two old friends mended fences, and the band regrouped to be inducted into the Rock and Roll Hall of Fame (which opened in Cleveland, Ohio, in 1995). They also released their first hit album in nearly a decade, *Steel Wheels*. Other accolades and awards followed for both the band and Jagger, including the ultimate honor for a native Englishman. In 2002, Mick Jagger was knighted by Queen Elizabeth II, becoming Sir Michael Philip Jagger.

GATHERING NO MOSS

Mick Jagger turned 60 in 2003. The press, which some say has rarely been fair to the Rolling Stones, has been critical because the Stones are older rock 'n' rollers who still tour and perform on stage. Pop-music critics tend to think that rock music is a young person's game. But the Stones are carrying on the tradition of the old blues artists like Muddy Waters, who never retired. Instead, these artists performed onstage and recorded new albums until death denied them another ovation. The only Stone to officially retire was bassist Bill Wyman in 1993. He was replaced with Chicagoan Darryl Jones. Throughout the 1990's and early 2000's, the Rolling Stones continued to release new albums, including the well-received *Voodoo Lounge* in 1994, *Bridges to Babylon* in 1997, and *A Bigger Bang* in 2005. They also continued to tour to promote the albums, selling out stadiums around the world. The Stones's 2006 performance during the nationally televised Super Bowl halftime show at Ford Field in Detroit—as well as their first performance in China that year—is further evidence that the band's popularity shows no sign of waning.

While other bands from the classic era of rock 'n' roll have returned to the stage to perform their old songs, Mick Jagger, Keith Richards, and the other Stones continue to compose and record new material. They insist on moving forward, finding new inspiration, and gaining new fans. ■

Jagger was knighted in 2002, becoming Sir Michael Philip Jagger. He is shown with his father, Joe Jagger, left, and two of his daughters. Karis (holding medal) is Jagger's daughter from a relationship with British actress Marsha Hunt. Elizabeth is Jagger's daugher with ex-wife, American actress and model Jerry Hall.

Notes

MUDDY WATERS

1. James Rooney, *Bossmen: Bill Monroe & Muddy Waters* (New York: Dial Press, 1971) 104.
2. Rooney 107.
3. Rooney 114.
4. Jas Obrecht, ed., *Blues Guitar: The Men Who Made the Music* (San Francisco: GPI Books, 1993) 91.
5. Rooney 145.
6. Obrecht 96.

ELVIS PRESLEY

Chapter 1

1. James Kingsley, "At Home With Elvis Presley," *Memphis Commercial Appeal, Mid-South Magazine*, 7 Mar. 1965, qtd. in Peter Guralnick, *Last Train to Memphis: The Rise of Elvis Presley* (Boston: Little, Brown and Co., 1994) 28.
2. Jerry Hopkins interview with Marion Keisker, 1970 (Mississippi Valley Collection at Memphis State University) qtd. in Guralnick 63.
3. *Time*, 14 May 1956, qtd. in Guralnick 64.
4. Guralnick 101.

Chapter 2

1. Ger J. Rijff, ed., *Long Lonely Highway: A 1950's Elvis Scrapbook* (Ann Arbor, Michigan: Pierian Press, 1987) 32.
2. Dave Marsh, *Elvis* (New York: Times Books, 1982) 100.
3. Press interview with Elvis Presley, 22 Sept. 1958, qtd. in Jerry Osborne, *Elvis: Word for Word* (New York: Harmony Books, 2000) 108.
4. Susan Doll, *Elvis: The Early Years* (Lincolnwood, Illinois: Publications International, Ltd., 1990) 58.
5. Rev. of *Love Me Tender, Time* 26 Nov. 1956: 106.

Chapter 3

1. Susan Doll, *Elvis: Forever in the Groove* (Lincolnwood, Illinois: Publications International, Ltd., 2003) 127.
2. "Elvis Aeternus," *Time* 19 June 1972: 50.

MICK JAGGER

1. Christopher Sandford, *Mick Jagger: Primitive Cool* (New York: St. Martin's Press, 1993) 17.
2. "Mick Jagger," *Current Biography*, 1972 ed., 238.
3. Sandford 57.
4. Sandford 68.
5. *Current Biography* 239.
6. Philip Norman, *Symphony for the Devil* (New York: Linden Press, 1984) 236.

Recommended Reading

BOOKS

Aldridge, John. *Satisfaction: The Story of Mick Jagger*. New York: Proteus, 1984.

Burk, Bill E. *Early Elvis: The Humes Years*. Memphis: Red Oak, 1990.

—. *Early Elvis: The Sun Years*. Memphis: Propwash, 1997.

—. *Early Elvis: The Tupelo Years*. Memphis: Propwash, 1994.

Cohn, Lawrence, ed. *Nothing but the Blues: The Music and the Musicians*. New York: Abbeville, 1993.

Cotten, Lee. *All Shook Up: Elvis Day-by-Day, 1954-1977*. Ann Arbor: Pierian Pr., 1985.

Davis, Stephen. *Old Gods Almost Dead: The 40-Year Odyssey of the Rolling Stones*. New York: Broadway Bks., 2001.

Doll, Susan M. *Understanding Elvis: Southern Roots vs. Star Image*. New York: Garland, 1998.

Gordon, Robert. *Can't Be Satisfied: The Life and Times of Muddy Waters*. Boston: Little, Brown, 2002.

Guralnick, Peter. *Careless Love: The Unmaking of Elvis Presley*. Boston: Little, Brown, 1999.

—. *Last Train to Memphis: The Rise of Elvis Presley*. Boston: Little, Brown, 1994.

Guralnick, Peter, and Ernst Jorgensen. *Elvis Day by Day*. New York: Ballantine, 1999.

Keogh, Pamela Clarke. *Elvis Presley: The Man, the Life, the Legend*. New York: Atria, 2004.

Norman, Philip. *The Stones: The Acclaimed Biography*. 2001. London: Pan, 2002.

Piazza, Jim. *The King*. New York: Black Dog & Leventhal, 2005.

Tooze, Sandra B. *Muddy Waters: The Mojo Man*. Toronto: ECW Pr., 1997.

WEB SITES

Elvis.com: The Official Site. Elvis Presley Enterprises, Inc. <http://www.elvis.com/>

Mickjagger.com. The Mick Jagger Website. <http://www.mickjagger.com/>

The Official Muddy Waters Website. Website is owned and produced by The Estate of McKinley Morganfield, aka Muddy Waters. <http://www.muddywaters.com/>

The Rock and Roll Hall of Fame and Museum <http://www.rockhall.com/>

"The Nixon-Presley Meeting, 21 December 1970." *The National Security Archive*. Gelman Library, The George Washington University. <http://www.gwu.edu/~nsarchiv/nsa/elvis/elnix.html>

Glossary

backbeat a percussion style in popular music where a strong rhythmic accent is sounded on the second and fourth beats of the bar.

big band a jazz band of 10 or more pieces. A big band consists of reed, brass, and rhythm sections.

blues a slow, melancholy song with jazz rhythm that originated among African Americans. It is usually in a major key but with the third and seventh (the blue notes) flatted optionally.

boogie-woogie (*BUG ee WUG ee* or *BOO gee WOO gee*) a form of blues played especially on the piano, marked by a repeating bass rhythm under a freely and elaborately varied, syncopated melody.

British Invasion the arrival in the United States of rock bands from England begun by the British rock group the Beatles in 1964.

Chicago blues a form of blues music that developed in Chicago, Illinois, by adding electric amplification, drums, piano, bass guitar, and sometimes saxophone, to the basic string/harmonica Delta blues.

country music a type of American popular music that developed in the southern United States during the 1800's. Country music combines elements of British and Anglo-American folk music, the blues, religious music, and popular songs. Country music is sometimes called country and western music.

Delta blues an emotional style of blues music that originated in the Mississippi Delta region, usually dominated by slide guitar and harmonica.

Dixieland a jazz style associated with New Orleans, marked by rapid tempo and lively improvisation.

doo-wop (*DOO wop*) rock 'n' roll group harmony music with a lead singer, especially popular in the 1950's and early 1960's.

field holler a short solo call or wail used as a form of communication among black plantation workers in the South.

gospel music music based on gospel songs, with elements of modern blues and jazz.

honky-tonk a cheap, low-class nightclub or dance hall or the kind of music played at such a place.

jazz a kind of music in which the accents fall at unusual places. It is native to the United States, where it developed from ragtime. The players slide from tone to tone, introduce independent tones, and imitate vocal effects with their instruments.

juke joint a tavern, roadhouse, or cheap cafe where music is furnished by a jukebox.

punk rock rock music performed in an aggressive, rowdy style.

rhythm and blues (r & b) rock 'n' roll with blues as its melodic element. R & b uses electrically amplified instruments rather than acoustic (nonelectric) guitars.

rock 'n' roll a kind of popular music with a strong beat and a simple, repetitious melody. It is played with two-beat rhythm that accents every second beat, usually with guitars and various other instruments for singing or dancing; rock. Rock 'n' roll is derived from folk music, blues, and jazz.

rockabilly (*ROK uh BIHL ee*) rock 'n' roll with hillbilly (country) music themes.

spiritual (*SPIHR uh chu uhl*) a religious song which originated among African Americans of the southern United States.

swing music a type of jazz for dancing, popular between about 1935 and 1944, in which the players improvise freely on the original melody.

syncopation (*SIHNG kuh PAY shuhn*) music, such as jazz or ragtime, marked by a shifting or anticipating of the accent to a normally unaccented beat.

Western swing a type of music which developed in Texas and Oklahoma combining country music with elements of big band jazz.

Index

Page numbers in *italic* type refer to pictures.